The Enneagram For Relationships

A Guide to Personality Types for Greater Self Discovery and Romance

Damian Blair

DISCLAIMER

No part of this publication may be reproduced, stored in a retrieval system or transmitted in any form or by any means, electronic, mechanical, photocopying, recording, scanning or otherwise except as permitted under Sections 107 or 108 of the 1976 United States Copyright Act, without the prior written permission of the publisher.

While every precaution has been taken in the preparation of this book, the publisher assumes no responsibility for errors or omissions, or for damages resulting from the use of the information contained herein.

This book is for entertainment and informational purposes only. The views expressed are those of the author alone and should not be taken as expert instruction or commands. The reader is responsible for his or her own actions. Neither the author nor the publisher assumes any responsibility or liability whatsoever on behalf of the purchaser or reader of these materials. The reader is responsible for their own use of any products or methods mentioned in this publication.

This book includes information about products and equipment offered by third parties. As such, the author does not assume responsibility or liability for any third party products or opinions. Third party product manufacturers have not sanctioned this book, nor does the author receive any compensation from said manufacturers for sharing information regarding their products.

Table of Contents

I. The Enneagram Types

4

II. Enneagram Pairings & Interplay

INTRODUCTION

When most people begin looking into the Enneagram and experimenting with how it can help them, they normally go straight to working on themselves. They may address their own weaknesses, shortcomings, or negative patterns of thinking and behavior. This is only natural. People tend to be more interested in themselves and their own personalities, how they think and view the world, and what makes them tick as a unique, individual person. Discovering your Enneagram type can have a very positive effect on a person, both for how they understand themselves, but also in what it reveals about how they relate to other people. Certain personalities complement each other in very positive and beneficial ways while others might more easily come to heads. Whatever the personality type, communication is the bedrock of any relationship, romantic or otherwise. Good communication can make it work whereas bad communication can destroy even those relationships that had such promising starts.

The Enneagram can give insight into what motivates each type, their particular triggers and irritations, and what to both build up and avoid in order to maintain a healthy relationship. For example, some types need very clear and straightforward communication while others are more comfortable with ambiguity. We will look at what each type needs when it comes to communication, how they can ask for what they want, and how they can affirm their own needs. Every Enneagram type is unique, and every type brings its own strengths, weaknesses, communication styles, and strange little idiosyncrasies to a relationship.

This book is not an introduction to the Enneagram, and it does not assume that the reader is a complete novice in the subject area. While some vocabulary and concepts will be reviewed briefly toward the beginning, they will not be discussed in any great detail. In the preface, we will briefly review the Enneagram itself: how it works, the levels of development in health and the directions of integration and disintegration, a short recap of each of the nine types, how the wings work and can influence a basic type, and a quick review on finding or confirming your own Enneagram type.

In Part I of this book, we will review each of the nine Enneagram types in more detail. While the basics were previously covered in *The Enneagram Beginner's Guide*, these chapters will delve deeper into several more comprehensive topics when it comes to the personality types and how they interact with others. We will look at the levels of development, or how each type integrates into health or disintegrates when they find themselves descending into stress. We will also look at how each type prefers to communicate, the degrees of intimacy with which they are comfortable, common types they mistake themselves for when deciphering their basic number, the nuances that either of the dominant wings can give to each type, and how to be accepting and affirming of each number. How to interact and communicate with each of the types can be especially helpful for those in a relationship to be aware of when it comes to how their partner's personality is structured.

In Part II, we will look at all of the possible pairings within the Enneagram. Each relationship is unique, but certain broad outlines can be drawn when looking at all of the basic types. How do Nines and Sevens interact in a relationship? How would a Three best communicate with a One? What type of communication style should a Four avoid when in a relationship with an Eight? And which should be embraced? Eliminating all conflict is an unattainable endeavor, but certain conflicts, altercations, and arguments can be avoided if partners are aware of what should be avoided with a particular Enneagram type. If you are aware of what might trigger your partner, and they are also aware of what might trigger you, then a good amount of negativity, disagreements, and resentment can be averted. This is especially true of things that can be triggering to a certain Enneagram type which someone else might have been completely unaware of. We will also look at the particular strengths of each type and how they can complement their partners. Conversely, we will also look at the areas each type needs to work on in order to improve themselves and their interpersonal relationships.

This book assumes that you already have a comfortable familiarity with the Enneagram, how it works, and the basics of what each of the nine personality types encompass. This is not an introductory book where all of the vocabulary, terminology, and elementary concepts are discussed apart from a concise review in the preface. This book is more concerned with how the Enneagram types interact with each other in the context of a romantic relationship. It is meant to help couples build a relationship and complement each other's strengths and weaknesses in constructive and beneficial ways. This is not a dating guide, nor is it an outline offering advice as to how to go about finding your ideal partner or perfect match based on which Enneagram type might theoretically be best for you.

The advice offered within these pages is not intended to be used to manipulate your partner in any way. When triggers are outlined for each type, they are meant to be avoided within the context of a healthy relationship. You should want the best for your partner, and they should want the best for you in return. The purpose of this book is to build, enhance, and solidify any romantic relationship in which you have taken part in order to create a more fulfilling connection. This in turn can ensure that you and your partner will have a better chance at a long and happy relationship.

I am a Two on the Enneagram, and my wife is a Seven; The Helper and The Enthusiast, respectively. Both of our types can have very different reactions to the same situation, as well as our own distinct feelings and emotional responses. In our relationship, we can both benefit from each other's weaknesses. She and I have to learn on our own how we best communicate, and then learn how to interact in the healthiest way with each other. For example, Twos such as myself can sometimes feel self-conscious and inhibited due to our core motivation of shame, but my Seven wife supports me with her outgoing attitude and endless pursuit of the next great adventure in life. In return, I can use my Two strengths to help her feel comfortable expressing her full range of emotions which she may have difficulty with doing on her own. Sevens are often uncomfortable with the less positive aspects of life, and Twos have the ability to put them at ease and feel both physically and emotionally safe. Each number on the Enneagram needs to talk through what they need from their partner, why they need it, and how they can work towards fulfilling each other's personal needs.

This book, *The Enneagram for Relationships*, is meant to be a guide to help couples discover both their own type further as well as those of their partner. Building a relationship is a long-term, perhaps even lifelong, process. Improved communication, understanding, empathy, and compassion can help both parties construct and fortify a more complementary relationship that can better withstand all of the difficulties that life can throw into their path. Good luck on the journey that you are undertaking together.

PREFACE

What Is the Enneagram? How Does it Work?

The Enneagram of Personality is a system meant to explain the nuances of human personality. It does this through the use of a visual diagram with nine points. On the surface, it looks simple and straightforward, but it has layers of meaning and understanding that can take a long time to decipher and implement in your own self-reflection. The term *enneagram* itself comes from the Greek word for *nine* (ennea) and *written* or *drawn* (gramma). Thus the word enneagram means *nine drawn* or *nine written*. The nine points on the Enneagram represent the nine basic types of human personality. The points of the Enneagram are divided into three centers. Each center includes three of the nine types, and they share a core motivation.

Sitting at the top of the diagram are the points representing the Eight, Nine, and One. These three numbers make up the Instinctive Center (sometimes also called the Body Center or the Gut Center). Although each type within a center is driven by the same basic motivator, it does not play out in the same way for each type. The three numbers of the Instinctive Center are driven by anger, but they are expressed very differently in each. The Eight lashes out in their anger, the Nine ignores it entirely, and the One turns it inward on themselves. As different as all of these approaches may be, anger is still the decisive motivator for the three types that make up the instinctive triad.

Further down and to the right of the Instinctive Center is the Feeling Center (sometimes also called the Heart Center). The thee numbers of the feeling triad are the Two, Three, and Four. They are all motivated in some way by shame. Twos are driven to prove their love to others by taking care of their most immediate needs. Threes work to prove their success to others in an attempt to suppress their shame. Fours are dedicated to proving how unique they are to the people around them in order to disprove their own sense of shame.

Going clockwise around the Enneagram, we come to the final center. The Thinking Center (sometimes also called the Head Center) includes the Five, Six, and Seven. These three types that make up the mental triad have fear as their main motivator. Fives are afraid of being inadequate or incapable of accomplishing what they set themselves to do. Sixes fear instability or the sensation of being unsafe. And Sevens are afraid of missing out on an experience or endeavor that is important or enjoyable, as well as of feeling pain.

Each of the nine types is located within its own center - Instinctive, Feeling, or Thinking - but each type is also divided into one of three stances. A stance describes how a personality interacts with other people, and how they set themselves up to relate to the world. The three stances are referred to as dependent, aggressive, and withdrawing. The One, Two, and Six are all dependent stances. They tend to move toward people in some way, and they look for guidance and validation outside of themselves and their own experiences. Of the three stances, the dependent types are the most focused on the present. They are also considered to be "thinking repressed." The Three, Seven, and Eight make up the three aggressive stances. Instead of moving toward people, the aggressive stance types move against them. The other six non-aggressive types often view them as hostile, but that is usually not their intention. They are simply driven to reach a certain goal that they have set for themselves, and they will do anything they can to achieve it. The aggressive stance types thrive on conflict and setting themselves against something in order to prove themselves. Whereas the dependent types focus on the present, the aggressive stance looks to the future. These three are also often viewed as "feeling repressed." Lastly we come to the withdrawing stance. The Four, Five, and Nine are the three assigned to this stance, and they prefer to move away from people. They tend to withdraw from the world and are more private than the other six types. The withdrawing types are considered to be "doing repressed" and center themselves around the past.

When listening to someone talk about the Enneagram, you might hear the term *wing*. A wing is simply the type to the left and right of a particular number. One or both of a number's wings will influence their personality in some way. For example, if you basic type is a Seven, you can have either a Six wing or an Eight wing. The Six is to the Seven's right and the Eight is to its left. Depending on how dominant either wing is, your Seven can be influenced and take on certain aspects of the Six or the Eight. A 7w6 (Seven wing Six) would come across quite differently from a 7w8 (Seven wing Eight). A Seven with an Eight wing would likely be more forceful, confident, and aggressive, whereas a more dominant Six wing could come across as more cautious, suspicious, or skeptical. Wings can also vary significantly, so some people may have a more even influence from their wings, and others might have an overpowering wing. A basic type can also lean into one or both of their wings at different times depending on which skills they might need in a particular moment or stage of life. A type Four might need the more proactive, driven, and ambitious skills from their Three wing at times, but at other times they may need the more introspective, measured, and thoughtful skills provided by their Five wings.

The nine personality types of the Enneagram are divided into both centers (Instinctive, Feeling, and Thinking) as well as stances (dependent, aggressive, and withdrawing). However, each type can also be further divided into something called the instinctual variant. This final aspect of the Enneagram adds to its complexity and dynamism. Instinctual variants are sometimes called simply instincts or even subtypes, although that is not, strictly speaking, an accurate term. The three instincts are Self-Preservation,

Social, and Sexual (sometimes also called One-to-One). Each Enneagram type can have any of the three instinctual variants, so there are a total of 27 different combinations of types and instinctual variants. You could be a Social Four or a Sexual Seven or a Self-Preservation Two. Everyone also has all three instincts within the makeup of their personality, but only one is the most dominant followed by their secondary instinct and then their least developed one. It is referred to as *stacking* when your instinctual variants are written out in their order of dominance. If you are an Eight with a dominant Social instinct followed by Sexual and then Self-Preservation, then you would write Eight so/sx. If you are a Five with a dominant Self-Preservation followed by Social instinct, then you would write Five sp/so. The least developed of the three instincts can be left off since we know which of the three is not listed.

The Self-Preservation instinct for any of the nine types is concerned with meeting their own immediate personal needs. They are preoccupied with their safety and level of comfort. However, they also concentrate their energy on having adequate resources for their everyday life, such as enough energy to complete their work or other tasks, enough money to pay their bills and live a comfortable life, or anything else that has to do with their daily life and any other immediate needs. Self-Preservation types are also often drawn to aesthetics like fashion, makeup, hair styling, home decor, and filling their spaces with things that they find beautiful or pleasing to look at. Of the three instinctual variants, Self-Preservation types are also the most introverted.

The Sexual instinct (sometimes also called One-to-One) is the most extroverted of the three. Sexual types are drawn to relationships of all kinds, not simply romantic ones. They are interested in the depth and energy that they receive and share in a relationship, whatever kind it might be. The Sexual types of any number pat attention to and are highly aware of the chemistry between themselves and other people. They can tell if their interpersonal communication is lacking in some way because they tend to want to merge with others. The Sexual instinct looks for intensity and is drawn specifically toward strong energy.

The Social instinctual variant is not necessarily a social butterfly. Even withdrawing stance types can have a dominant Social instinct. Social types are aware of the people around them, and they are highly adaptable to new situations. They can be chameleons, subtly or even dramatically changing the ways in which they interact with other people depending on where they are and what they are doing. They might behave in a substantially different manner depending on if they are at a big event for work or a small, intimate dinner party. Social types desire a personal connection, so they adapt themselves to whatever is necessary to the situation in order to achieve that goal. They place importance on finding meaningful experiences to share with the people in their lives.

While not officially part of the Enneagram of Personality, tritypes have become a popular term in many online Enneagram communities. The idea of the tritype is that you have a dominant type within each center. In the Instinctive Center, you would have a dominant Eight, Nine, or One. In the Feeling Center, you would have a stronger Two, Three, or Four. And in the Thinking Center, you would have a more dominant Five, Six, or Seven. Your overall dominant number is your basic type along with your stronger wing. However, you would also have a dominant number within each of the other two centers, although they would obviously be weaker than your basic type.

For example, if you dominant type is Five with a Four wing, you would be a 5w4. But then within the Feeling Center, you might have a stronger Two along with a stronger Eight in the Instinctive Center. You would thus write your tritype as 528 if your order of dominance is Five, Two, and Eight. Or you would write it as 582 if your order of dominance is rather Five, Eight, and Two. The idea is that you have a stronger type within each center that can influence your personality in some way. As with wings, it does not mean that that type determines or changes your basic type. It only influences it to some degree. In this example, you would have a Four wing to your Five, but you would not *be* a Four. Similarly, you would have a dominant Two in your Feeling Center and a dominant Eight in your Instinctive Center, but you would not *be* a Two or an Eight.

Levels of Development

One of the most helpful aspects of the Enneagram is that you can trace your own development as you move through the levels of health. Originally developed by Don Richard Riso and Russ Hudson, nine levels of health can be applied to each of the basic types. Most people, whatever their type is, tend to operate in the average range of health (Riso and Hudson, 1999).

Healthy
  * Levels 1, 2 and 3

Average
  * Levels 4, 5 and 6

Unhealthy
  * Levels 7, 8 and 9

The best way to track your own development is to discover your basic type. Once you know this, you can look at the distinctive pathway of both integration to health and disintegration to stress that each type follows. For example, Twos move toward Eight when they are stressed and disintegrating. This means that they can take on certain aspects of the behavior and temperament of an Eight. It does not mean that they *become* an Eight. On the other hand, Twos move toward Four when they are integrating into health. They take on the positive traits and aspects of the Four when they move into the healthy range of their personality type.

Again, they do not *become* a Four; they simply take on the health traits of the Four.

Each of the nine Enneagram types has their own unique pathway toward integration and disintegration. This is how you can track your own personal level of health and how you handle stress.

Disintegration into Stress

- One takes on the negative traits of Four
- Two takes on the negative traits of Eight
- Three takes on the negative traits of Nine
- Four takes on the negative traits of Two
- Five takes on the negative traits of Seven
- Six takes on the negative traits of Three
- Seven takes on the negative traits of One
- Eight takes on the negative traits of Five
- Nine takes on the negative traits of Six

Integration into Health

- One takes on the positive aspects of Seven
- Two takes on the positive aspects of Four
- Three takes on the positive aspects of Six
- Four takes on the positive aspects of One
- Five takes on the positive aspects of Eight
- Six takes on the positive aspects of Nine
- Seven takes on the positive aspects of Five
- Eight takes on the positive aspects of Two
- Nine takes on the positive aspects of Three

The Nine Personality Types

Communication is key to any relationship. It is how people express themselves, what they want, what they need, how they are feeling, if they are hurt or happy, and how their partner should respond to them. The Enneagram teaches that there are nine basic personality types, along with many variations on them, that all communicate in different ways. Some prefer more structured and organized methods of conversation and communication. Others rely more on their emotions and unspoken communication. Some types are very direct, whereas other types may take such directness as annoyance when it was not intended in that way. Other types are not very communicative verbally, which the more direct types may take as resentment or ambivalence when it was not meant to be taken that way.

When couples learn their Enneagram types, they can begin to see how and why they function the way they do, as well as why their partner thinks and acts the way they do. All of the types are quite diverse in how they take in and process information, as well as how they respond to their partners or other people in their lives. Learning how the people you love communicate, as well as what works and does not work for them in this context, can help build trust, peace, harmony, sympathy, and empathy. Without proper and compassionate communication, a relationship will eventually fall apart.

Type One is known as The Reformer or The Perfectionist. A One with a Nine wing is often referred to as The Idealist, and a One with a Two wing is called The Advocate. They have a dependent stance, so they prefer to move toward people rather than away or against. Ones are also located in the Instinctive Center, so they are driven in some way by anger. However, they do not normally view anger as an acceptable emotion, so they suppress and deny it, turning it inward on themselves rather than expressing it for the people around them to see. Ones have a strong sense of ethics and are drawn to black-and-white thinking. Reformers see the world as split between right and wrong, good and bad, with very little gray area between. They strive to be ethical, just, and right. Ones are very orderly and organized, and they work to achieve the highest possible personal standard in every aspect of their lives.

Ones that have become unhealthy can be rigid, dogmatic, and unbending. They are often overly critical of everyone but most especially themselves. Because they are so committed to perfection, both inside and out, they can turn that perpetual tendency toward criticism loose on their interpersonal relationships. Ones with Ones may not present much of a difficulty with this, but other types do not handle constant critiques and criticism so well. It is important for Ones to pursue peace rather than perfection in their relationships. Their basic fear that they are corrupt, imperfect, or lacking in some intrinsic way must be softened and instead directed only at themselves rather than at the other people in their lives. Then they will be free to go after their basic desire in life of finding a personal sense of honor and a harmonious balance within both themselves and their relationships

Type Two is nicknamed The Helper or sometimes The Giver. Twos with a One wing are called The Servant, and those with a Three wing are known as The Host or The Hostess. As one of the members of the dependent stance, Twos move toward other people as they go through life. They want to express their love and appreciation for others, but they also want to receive it back in return. Twos also make up part of the Feeling Center, which are all driven in some way by shame. Twos are empathetic, exude warmth in their personal interactions, and are usually very friendly and outgoing. They live to be of service to others. Part of the reason Twos seek to take care of others' needs is to counteract their own sense of unworthiness. They try to prove to both themselves and others that the shame they feel is not actually there. Unhealthy Twos feel that they must be loved, needed, and receive affirmation and affection for what they have sacrificed. Their self-sacrifice can turn into martyrdom when they descend into the lower levels of their health. In every relationship, Twos often have a hard time communicating what it is they need or want. They often ignore their own needs, even basic ones, to the point that their health can suffer. Twos need to be aware of this so that they do not eventually give into resentment towards the people they love. At their core, Twos fear that they are not worthy of the love they seek in life. They are afraid of being unwanted and disposable. Twos must learn to trust in the people they love that they will not be abandoned. It is then that they can realize their desire to find love, acceptance, and appreciation.

Type Three is called The Achiever or The Performer. Threes with a Two wing are known as The Charmer, and those with a Four wing are referred to as The Professional. As one of the aggressive stances, they move against people and are one of the more extroverted types on the Enneagram. They are also located in the Feeling Center, but they approach their shame in a different way from Twos. Whereas Twos try to prove their love to others, Threes work to prove their success. Threes are very concerned with image and how they present themselves to the world, as well as their own success and status in life. Achievers are ambitious, driven, and motivated to succeed in every aspect of their lives, from personal to professional and everything that may lie in between. Twos know their shame is there, and they seek to disprove it. Threes ignore and suppress that shame entirely. They focus themselves on succeeding at any and all cost.

When Threes become unhealthy, they can give into their obsession with image, status, and the appearance of success when that might not be accurate. Above all, Threes are afraid of being worthless, so they throw themselves into everything they do. Work often takes centerstage in the life of a Three in an effort to prove how valuable and essential they are. Threes must be irreplaceable, but their downfall is that they often associate their success so closely with their value as a person that they disassociate themselves from their emotions. Their work life may also run into their personal life with no real visible boundaries. This tendency toward being a workaholic can make a Three's partner feel as though they hold second place in their life and priorities. By focusing on the present rather than the future-oriented aggressive stance, Threes can find their sense of value as an individual person, become more comfortable with their emotions, and learn to view that work as both worthwhile and only one part of the skills and talents they have to offer.

Type Four is known as The Individualist or The Tragic Romantic. Those with a Three wing are commonly referred to as The Aristocrat, and Fours with a Five wing are called The Bohemian. Fours are said to be the rarest of the nine Enneagram types, and they are also the most complex. They are one of the withdrawing stances, so they are generally very reserved and introverted. Fours tend to move away from people rather than toward or against as the other two stances do. As members of the emotional triad, Fours are also driven in some way by shame. While Twos deal with their shame by proving their love to others and Threes by proving their success to others, Fours go about proving how singularly uncommon they are to the people around them. They are drawn to uniqueness and authenticity, both for themselves personally and in everything that they might undertake. Fours pursue creativity and honesty in every aspect of their lives. Many are artists of some kind or find other creative endeavors or outlets in their work.

When Fours descend into the unhealthy regions of their personality, they can become self-conscious, overly critical of themselves, and wallow in melancholy or even depression. Above all, Fours are afraid that they have no identity or that they lack authenticity. They often convince themselves that there is something wrong with them, that they can never have a normal relationship or connect on a personal level with anyone. Because of this, Fours often envy those around them. They want what other people have found, and this can lead them to turn a blind eye to the possible relationships that they already have in their life. Fours are motived by their search to discover themselves and find the key to their own happiness.

When they are true to themselves, accept themselves and all of their messy emotions and shortcomings, they can more easily accept the love of another person.

Type Five is The Investigator or The Observer. Fives with a Four wing are commonly known as The Iconoclast, and those with a Six wing are called The Problem Solver. As with Fours, Fives are also a withdrawing stance. They are normally quite introverted and prefer to spend huge amounts of time on their own reading, researching, or otherwise accumulating large amounts of knowledge and information. Fives are also located in the Thinking Center, which is motivated by fear. Fives are drawn to intellectual pursuits, complex thoughts and ideas, and a drive to find knowledge and understanding. They want to comprehend both themselves and the world on a profound, analytical level. Fives are usually very independent and can easily view situations and find solutions outside of the proverbial box.

When unhealthy, Fives can sometimes have the tendency to retreat too far into their minds and find themselves overcome by their own thoughts and fears. Their insecurities can take hold of them and refuse to let go. Those that have descended into an unhealthy space can come across as eccentric and even nihilistic. More than anything, Fives are afraid of being useless or helpless. This is one reason they are so devoted to their pursuit of information and knowledge. They want it to be easily accessible in order to help them cope with the pressure of life. Their intellectualism is meant to remedy and counteract their fear of being an incompetent member of their community. Fives need this huge amount of alone-time to decompress, prepare themselves for social encounters, and learn how to interact with the world and other people from an analytical perspective. Neither Fives nor their partners might know that they need to find balance between self-care (usually a lot of time spent alone for a Five) and social interactions. Once they are able to find this balance in their relationships, they can then see themselves as productive and competent individuals in their society and generous and thoughtful partners in their relationship.

Type Six, known as The Loyalist or The Trooper, is perhaps the most common of all the types on the Enneagram, at least in North America. A Six with a Five wing is called The Defender, and a Six with a Seven wing is referred to as The Buddy. Sixes are a dependent stance, so they move toward people as opposed to away or against. This manifests in the importance they place on groups, structure, and teamwork. They are not individualists in the sense that they prefer to do everything on their own without outside help or input. As with Fives, Sixes are motivated by fear. However, Sixes tend to be afraid of fear itself. They will often play through worst case scenarios in their head just to be prepared for any possible misfortune. Security and stability are of paramount importance to the Six, for both themselves and society. They believe in cooperation and teamwork, and they are the most reliable and loyal of all the Enneagram numbers.

When Sixes become unhealthy, they can become very stressed, anxious, and even paranoid. They can find it difficult to make decisions and have little faith in their own talents and abilities. More than anything else, Sixes value security. They like to know what to expect, so they do not usually appreciate surprises. Sixes often worry a lot, and part of that worry has to do with their relationships. Human interactions of all kinds can be messy and unpredictable, and Sixes in particular do not like this. They worry that the people in their lives might not always be there for them. Sixes must learn to let go of their fear of change. They must remember that while change is inevitable, negativity is not. Sixes have to learn to trust themselves and the people they love. Once they do this, they can find a sense of the stability that they have sought for so long.

Type Seven is The Enthusiast or The Epicure. Sevens with a Six wing are referred to as The Entertainer, and those with an Eight wing are called The Realist. Sevens are one of the three aggressive stances, so they move against people rather than toward or away. Their endless pursuit of the new and exciting can be intimidating to others and perhaps even rub them the wrong way. In addition to being an aggressive stance, Sevens are also located in the Thinking Center. They are motivated by fear, which could be either the fear of pain itself, somber emotions, or just an unpleasant experience of some kind. Sevens are so drawn to positivity that they can shun everything else in life that does not measure up to their expectations. They have a nearly endless amount of optimism and are enthusiastic about living life to the fullest. Sevens are adaptable and usually have no problem with a last-minute change of plans. They prefer to live spontaneously in the moment, and they are always looking for the next adventure or new thing to experience.

An unhealthy Seven can become dangerously impulsive, and they also ignore unpleasant tasks or experiences. A boring or uninspiring task can be left uncompleted because the Seven cannot be bothered to complete it because of their preference for positive, pleasant, and invigorating experiences. Their basic fear is of experiencing pain or unpleasant situations, so they are always on the move, running from the things they do not wish to experience and toward the things they do not want to miss out on. Sevens can become very flighty, living in the future and always pursuing the next project, to the point that the people in their lives might begin to feel that they are not good enough. It seems to them that their companionship is not valued by the Seven. Instead of always running after the next great experience, Sevens should learn to be present, enjoying the people they are with at the moment, and valuing every shared experience.

Type Eight is known as The Challenger or The Boss. Those with a Seven wing are called The Maverick, and Eights with a Nine wing are referred to as The Bear. Along with Threes and Sevens, Eights are one of the three aggressive stances. Perhaps more so than the other two types, Eights most obviously move against people. They can thrive on conflict and aggression, but it is important to realize that these more aggressive tendencies of theirs are not meant to be taken personally. It is just how they are most comfortable communicating and expressing themselves. Eights are also one of the three members of the Instinctive Center. They are motivated by anger at their core, and they are very comfortable with expressing that anger. They do not repress this emotion or turn it inward as the other two members of the instinctive triad are known to do. They are the most assertive and even aggressive type on the Enneagram. Eights are not afraid to voice their opinion, stand up for what they believe in, or advocate for what they think is right. At their best, they are straightforward and confident in themselves. However, when an Eight descends into the unhealthy regions of their personality type, they can become particularly destructive. They can lash out at others, bully the people around them, and sometimes even resort to physical aggression.

Eights do not appreciate the sensation of vulnerability, so they will turn the tables and make others feel vulnerable in their place. Their basic fear is of being controlled by others. Eights prefer to control themselves, their surroundings, and their lives, and they do not take kindly to others attempting to usurp control, even within the context of a romantic relationship. Eights are perhaps the most independent of all the Enneagram types, and are extremely action-oriented. This can perhaps feel aggressive to their partner, especially when their opinions are not taken into consideration. Eights would do well to take a step back and weigh any options with the person or people their decisions might affect. While Eights do not like the sensation of vulnerability, and they desire to protect themselves from the possibility of being controlled by any outside force, when Eights can put their thoughts and motives into words and include others in their lives, this sense of shared vulnerability will help their relationships grow.

Type Nine is The Peacemaker or The Mediator. Nines with an Eight wing are commonly known as The Referee, and those with a One wing are called The Dreamer. Nines, along with Fours and Fives, are one of the withdrawing stances. They move away from people and prefer to spend a large amount of time alone. This is where their value of peace, harmony, and relaxation really comes into play. Many Nines are quite introverted homebodies who enjoy spending time at home on their own. As a member of the Instinctive Center, Nines are motivated by anger. However, they express it in a very different way from the Eight or the One. Eights can have explosive anger and Ones repress it, turning it inward on themselves. Nines completely deny the anger is even present. They do not want to deal with the negative and unharmonious experience of such a dark emotion. They are the most relaxed and easygoing of all the types on the Enneagram, as well as the least complex. Nines value peace, cooperation, and harmony. They tend to avoid conflict at almost any cost, to the point that they can often fall asleep to their own needs and desires. This is when the Nine can descend into being an unhealthy example of their type. They can become complacent in their fear of initiating a conflict or altercation of some kind, even one that is necessary to their mental wellbeing. A Nine might put off ending a relationship or quitting a job, both of which might be destructive to them in some way, because they don't want to rock the boat and disrupt both their own and others' peace of mind.

At their core, Nines fear losing their connection with other people. This is why they value peace and harmony. They prefer not to risk any form of conflict, which in turn might hurt a relationship. Nines are also skilled at seeing all sides of a situation or conflict, even one in which they are involved. Because of these tendencies, Nines often do not stand up for themselves or articulate their opinions. Nines need to remember that true peace and harmony can only be attained when they are also happy with what they have fought for and attained. Nines who have stepped into their ability to assert themselves are able to have greater peace in both their lives and their minds.

How to Find Your Type

Discovering your own unique type can prove to be a difficult endeavor, and it is very common to mistype yourself. If you have no familiarity with the Enneagram, then you could begin with taking a handful of online tests to narrow down your possible types. You could have more of an inclination toward the withdrawing stances, so you would then score more highly on types Four, Five, and Nine. From there, you can begin to narrow down which of the three fits you best. Or you might have a similar experience with the aggressive or dependent stances.

When you take a series of online tests, you should keep track of which types keep popping up in your results. You can also pay attention to which types you consistently receive lower scores on because those can be eliminated. From there, you should be able to narrow down your types to perhaps three or four possibilities. If you have somewhat more of a familiarity with the Enneagram, perhaps if you have read a book or followed some social media accounts, then perhaps you have already narrowed yourself down to two or three types. At this point, it would be a good idea to read up on those few types that you think describe you best. If you are caught between types Eight and Three, read further into their personality traits and especially their inner motivations. Why do they do what they do? What is their core motivation? Both Eight and Three are aggressive stances, so they can sometimes appear to be very similar. But Eights are driven by anger and Threes are motivated by shame. These two types have very different reasons for behaving the way they do. This is your biggest clue into what your true Enneagram number is.

Once you have narrowed down your possible types to somewhere between perhaps two and four, you should read up on all of them and decide which descriptions fit you best. It is important to look at more than just outward behavior or aspects of your personality that are readily apparent. Types can look similar to each other, especially if they have the same stance or are integrating into health or disintegrating into stress. The Enneagram deals with your core motivation and what drives you at your core. This is also why it is so difficult, if not impossible, to accurately guess others' Enneagram types. No one else knows what exactly drives you internally.

I. The Enneagram Types

ONE: The Reformer

Levels of Health and Development

When Ones are moving into the healthier regions of their personality, they take on the playful and spontaneous qualities of Sevens. They are better able to handle the unexpected changes that daily life brings. Healthy Ones become more flexible and receptive to changes in everyday life as well as to how the dynamic of their relationships might be altered. Those Ones that are on the lower average end of the scale or even descending into the unhealthy parts of their personality can be extremely rigid and unwilling to see the world from another point of view. In their opinion, only their way is the correct method of doing something. Most Ones that have not approached integration are at least somewhat obsessed with doing absolutely everything the correct way. Following directions or the perceived right way to do something is of paramount importance to the One. If something is done only partially, they will often feel annoyance and resentment over their perceived lack of focus, initiative, or follow-through. Unhealthy Ones' rigidity often permeates into every aspect of their lives to the point that they might drive people away from them due to their constant criticism and nitpicking.

Healthy: Levels 1, 2, and 3

- Ones in this region are at their best. They are able to retain their deep sense of right and wrong, their moral principles, and their personal ethics and morality while also accepting what is realistically possible and becoming less rigid. Healthy Ones realize that the world is not always black and white, and they are more able to acknowledge and affirm all of its nuances.

Average: Levels 4, 5, and 6

- Average Ones tend to have some sense of dissatisfaction with how things are, and they often turn to advocacy of some kind to attain their idealistic visions of what could be. As they descend further toward their unhealthy levels, they can become more unbending and even angry at what they see as failing to live up to their high expectations.

Unhealthy: Levels 7, 8, and 9

- Unhealthy Ones can become inflexible and intolerant. They are obsessed with their own perfection as well as the mistakes of others. These Ones can also become very judgmental and hypocritical.

Communication

Ones tend to be very direct in their communication style. They like to know what to expect, both from themselves and from others. In their professional and personal lives, Ones are very diligent, organized, and focused on doing their best. They want to prove themselves as being right, good, and just in every aspect of their lives and achieve their highest potential. Everything must be, not merely good enough, but to the absolute best of their ability. This is where the moniker The Perfectionist comes from. Good enough for everyone else is not good enough for a perfectionist. However, as hard as they might be on other people for not living up to their expectations, Ones are even harder on themselves. They have a constant inner voice that tells them that what they are doing is not their best and must be redone until it is. Ones are very critical of themselves, and this in turn makes them critical of others. Their criticism is not meant to wound; it is meant to improve. The problem is that not every type is so focused on endless improvements. Some just want to get the task or endeavor completed. Perfection is not of paramount importance to everyone. Ones must learn that not everyone handles criticism with as much positivity as they do. They should remember that criticism must be tempered with compliments. Ones also appreciate very direct communication. They want to know up front what is expected of them and what the parameters might be within a relationship.

Intimacy

Ones are very hard on themselves because they can never seem to adequately measure up in their own eyes. It is difficult for them to let their insecurities go and allow themselves to be vulnerable with another person. Their inner voice constantly criticizes them, what they do, and who they are to the point that they can become rigid and fragile. Criticism or negativity of any kind needs to be tempered with positive reassurance like compliments or praise. Instead of only saying what has gone wrong or is not working, preface such statements with what is good or what has gone well. Any negative response, even minor or implied, can put a One on edge and even raise their anger. When a One feels safe and secure, sensing that their efforts have been put to good effect, the lack of perfection in every area is then acceptable to them.

Common Mistypes

Mistyping your own Enneagram number is quite common. Ones and Threes can sometimes be mistyped because both are very organized and driven by success. However, success means something different to these two types. Threes want tangible success - achievements, wealth, possessions, etc. - and Ones are more drawn to perfection. They want success on their own terms. Another of the biggest differences between these two is that Ones are unwilling to take shortcuts or cut corners to attain their goal. Threes are more than willing to do so. The end goal is more important to the Three whereas every step in the process is of equal importance to the One.

Ones can also mistype themselves as either a Nine or a Two by misidentifying one of their wings as their basic type. If one or the other wing is particularly dominant, or they recognize certain traits of their wing on a regular basis, the One could mistype themselves as one of those wings. Similarly, Ones could also misidentify themselves as a Four. This occurs most often when a One is particularly unhealthy and has taken on the more negative traits of a type Four. Ones disintegrate in the direction of Four when they become stressed. While not as common, Ones that are very healthy might also type themselves as a Seven because they have taken on so many of the positive qualities of The Enthusiast.

Wing Personalities

Ones can have either a Nine wing or a Two wing. The Idealist (1w9) is more focused on the big-picture, rather than minute details. Like Nines, they can see all sides of every conflict or opinion, and they seek to build bridges and find common ground between them. Ones with a stronger Nine wing are less focused on being right or good than on finding peace between opposing viewpoints. They are more able to relax and let things go, whereas a One with a weaker connection to a Nine is more focused on being correct and can become preoccupied with what they see as having been done wrong or incorrectly. The Advocate (1w2) is able to lean into their wing's Heart Center, so they have more access to their emotions. Advocates do not repress their feelings, including their anger, as much as other Ones are known to do. These Ones have more access to empathy, and they care deeply about the people in their lives. Like Twos, they show more of a commitment to help those in need and connect with others on a deeper level.

Acceptance

Ones are very critical of themselves, and even when healthy, they can be somewhat rigid in their beliefs and how they deal with themselves and others. While Ones often criticize the people with whom they interact, usually out of a desire to attain the highest level of quality in whatever project or endeavor is being perfected, they are even more critical of themselves. It is important to accept Ones for always having the desire to improve the world around them. Doing something poorly or only partway is not in their vocabulary, and it would put an added stressor onto their psyche. But it is also important to help Ones temper their perfectionism with acceptance, especially when it comes to accepting themselves personally. No one is perfect, not even a perfectionist, and no one can do everything perfectly all the time. It is an unattainable endeavor. With Ones, it is important to emphasize that doing your personal best is not only good enough, but it is perfect enough. Because Ones often work so hard to attain a standardized perfection in both their personal and professional lives, it is important to help them step back and realize that their personal best is good enough for them. It is also essential to encourage Ones to rest and relax from time to time, and ideally at regular intervals.

TWO: The Helper

Levels of Health and Development

When Twos integrate into their personality's healthy range, they move toward type Four. They are able to become more comfortable and at ease with their darker, more melancholic feelings and embrace the full range of their emotions. These integrating Twos are able to focus on their own needs rather than constantly looking after and serving others. They are able to become more centered, aware of how they feel and what they need to do for themselves. Healthy Twos often find a creative outlet for their newfound comfort with expressing their own feelings. On the other hand, when Twos becomes stressed and begin their path toward disintegration, they take on many of the characteristics of type Eight. Eights are known for being controlling, aggressive, and domineering. When Twos are not shown the affection or attention that they feel they deserve, they can take on these more aggressive traits. They may become possessive, demanding, and attempt to control the people around them.

Healthy: Levels 1, 2, and 3

- Twos in these three levels are at their healthiest. They are full of empathy and compassion for others, and they show unconditional love to the people around them. While very focused on others and what they need, healthy Twos are also aware of their own needs. Service is done because they love others and it brings them joy, not because they hope to get anything in return for it.

Average: Levels 4, 5, and 6

- Average Twos can begin to engage in people-pleasing behaviors. They have ulterior motives to all of the love, care, and affection they bestow on others. They flatter others in order to receive the affirmation and affection they need. As they descend lower into stress, Twos can intrude inappropriately into others' lives and force their possessive affection on them.

Unhealthy: Levels 7, 8, and 9

- Unhealthy Twos often try to use guilt to manipulate others into doing or feeling things for them. They want sympathy, appreciation, acknowledgement, and affection, and they resort to destructive tactics in order to attain them. At their most unhealthy, Twos can develop a victim complex which breeds a sense of bitterness and resentment with which they continue to lash out at others.

Communication

Twos are very affectionate people. They are warm, kind, and caring. These qualities shine through in how they they tend to communicate with people. Twos are driven by their desire to love others and put them at ease in their presence. One way they accomplish this is through compliments. They want the people around them to know how much they are appreciated. A Two will notice the way you have styled your hair, changed your makeup, or how a color accentuates your eyes. They will let you know how nice it looks on you. Just as much as they enjoy giving out this positive reinforcement, they also want to receive it back from others. As much as Twos go out of their way to acknowledge what the people around them need, they also want those in their personal or professional sphere to return the favor. Twos will also give positive feedback or constructive criticism in the hopes that they can build others up and gently push them toward their best. They are excellent listeners, and they will often seek out those who seem uncomfortable or out of place in order to initiate a conversation. If even one person is not at ease, the Two won't be either. Because they are so oriented toward others, Twos will use a lot of second-person pronouns. "How are you doing?" "What are you up to?" "What do you feel like doing?" The conversation is often more centered on the person they are talking to rather than on themselves. And these are generally not superficial conversations; the Two is genuinely interested in knowing how you are doing and what you are up to.

Intimacy

Twos are much more concerned with what others need than with what they need. This is true when they are at both their healthiest and unhealthiest, although the reasons are different for both. However, they do not know what they need. This is true for them in any kind of relationship, from romantic to personal to professional. Because Twos are in the Feeling Center, they often take action or do favors for other people with the sense that it will be reciprocated. But other types, especially those in the Thinking Center or Instinctive Center, would not necessarily feel the same way. This can become particularly problematic because Twos will often not articulate what they are thinking or what they mean in this respect. Those in a relationship with a Two should make it a point to ask them what their motives and intentions are and help them put into words what it is they need or want.

Common Mistypes

Mistyping yourself happens frequently, especially for those who are new to the Enneagram. Twos and Sixes are a somewhat common misidentification. Both types are social, outgoing, and truly enjoy the company of other people. However, a major difference between the two is that Sixes want acceptance and approval while Twos want acceptance and love. Sixes are also drawn toward an authority figure or force of some kind, whereas Twos are content without such outside influence. Twos and Sevens can also be mistaken for each other for similar reasons. While both types love being around people and building relationships with them, they have slightly different motives. Twos want a deep relationship, and they focus on an intimate level of warmth, care, and concern. Sevens are not as interested in the depth or intimacy of their friendships or other relationships. They do not like doing many activities alone, but they don't tend to care who they are with whether it be close friends or casual acquaintances (so long as they are not alone).

Twos can also misidentify themselves as either a One or a Three if they mistake themselves for one or the other of their wings. This can happen especially if one wing is very dominant, and they can become confused between their basic type and their stronger wing. In a similar way, Twos could also mistake themselves for being an Eight if they happen to be descending into stress or even in one of the unhealthier regions of their personality type. They also integrate toward type Four when they are at their healthiest. It is possible for a Two to mistake themselves as an Eight or a Four because those two types are their pathways of disintegration and integration, respectively. It is also worth noting that women often mistype themselves as Twos.

Type Twos are very "others-oriented" and focused on serving, and these traits tend to be valued and reinforced to a much higher degree in women than men. It is common for women of other types to misidentify themselves as Twos. If you are a woman who has scored highly or even the highest in type Two, also look at your next highest scores to be sure of your type.

Wing Personalities

Twos can have either a One wing or a Three wing. The Servant (2w1) tends to be more concerned with being correct (or just) than The Host or The Hostess (2w3) might be. Twos with a Three wing tend to be more social and outgoing than the 2w1. Since both their basic number and dominant wing are located in the Feeling Center, they have even more access to their feelings and are less reserved about expressing them. The 2w1 is more concerned with altruism, and their concerns may turn to social justice and working to improve their own community, or perhaps even implementing a better vision of the world. Servants are generous people who approach others with warmth, care, and genuine concern. Hosts and Hostesses are usually more outgoing and social. They enjoy planning and organizing social endeavors and getting to know people at the parties and events that they have put together.

Acceptance

Twos are extremely others-oriented. While they are astutely aware of what those around them need, and this is especially true when it comes to their romantic partner, they are not necessarily aware of what they need for themselves. Twos often find it difficult to clearly articulate what it is they want, need, or expect from a relationship. They often use the small (or large) favors they do for others as a way to communicate what they are looking for. Most Twos are probably not consciously aware that this is what they are doing when they engage in this type of behavior. Twos are very dependent on others, especially when it comes to their romantic relationship. They need affirmation, not for any ego-boosting reasons, but rather because they need to feel loved and appreciated. Without this type of support, a Two's sense of self can suffer. They are very generous people who put others before themselves even when they are unhealthy. Others can find this trait easy to take advantage of, so it is of paramount importance for Twos to be supporters and accepted for who they are rather than what they can give within a relationship. The truth that they are not merely the kind deeds they do for others must be reinforced, and that they are loved for themselves alone rather than for the good that they take joy in doing for others.

THREE: The Achiever

Levels of Health and Development

When Threes integrate into health, they take on the positive traits of the type Six. They focus themselves on how they relate to the people around them rather than being so concerned with what they need to do and the goals or tasks they need to accomplish in order to be successful in their own eyes. Healthy Threes also become less competitive and instead work for the betterment of others, building up the people around them whom they no longer view as their competition. These Threes are more cooperative with everyone in their lives - romantic, personal, and professional - and have a better ability to show real commitment within all of their relationships. When a Three disintegrates, they move toward Nine and take on many of the negative characteristics of that type. Unhealthy Nines are characterized by their apathy, lethargy, and becoming disengaged from the activities in their lives. These Threes can become obsessed with completing tasks simply for the sake of finishing something. This could take the form of busywork that is completely unessential to their lives. Unhealthy Threes lose the sense of optimism and confidence that normally characterizes The Achiever.

Healthy: Levels 1, 2, and 3

- Threes in this range are at their best. They are sure of themselves, full of energy, and intent on improving themselves for their own sake. These Threes are highly competent and accept themselves as they are.

Average: Levels 4, 5, and 6

- Average Threes can become consumed with performing. They want to put their best foot forward and make sure their image is as highly manicured as possible. They can become obsessed with impressing others with how good, successful, or talented they are. They rely more on others' expectations of them rather than their own expectations for themselves.

Unhealthy: Levels 7, 8, and 9

- Threes who have descended into the lower regions of their personality type are consumed by the fear that they will fail in their endeavors. They will often go to any length to preserve their image of success. These unhealthy Threes often view others as competition and treat them as such.

Communication

Threes are chameleons. They have the ability to dramatically adapt themselves to nearly any person or situation. They cover up their fears and insecurities by donning the mask they think will bring them the most ease at that particular moment. If they need to be outgoing and sociable, that is how they will behave. If they need to pull it back and be somber, they can do that too. The Three often does not communicate their own needs or desires, but rather those that they think will be acceptable in any given situation. Although the Three might seem comfortable and sure of themselves, they may not be within. Threes are also often unaware of their own feelings because they often suppress or ignore them. It is important to talk through how an Achiever might be feeling in a certain situation and work through what might be going on with them subconsciously. Even though the Three is a member of the Feeling Center, their emotional displays are not as readily apparent as the Two or the Four. However, it is just as important that they get in touch with how their emotions might be affecting them. Threes tend to be much more comfortable with more positive emotions, and they will often communicate using a lot of exclamation points, happy emojis, cheerful words, and excited greetings and sign-offs. They are one of the aggressive stances, and this makes them very future-oriented. Threes are often described as being proactive, optimistic, active, and always looking forward to what is coming next. When they make mistakes, they prefer to focus on how to make improvements to positively affect the future rather than dwelling on the more negative aspects of the past.

Intimacy

Threes are so driven by their pursuit of success that they can shut down their emotions and ability to relate to other people on a deeper level. The depth of their inner world may be sacrificed to an extent in favor of a sort of superficiality that they think will be more appealing to a wider range of people. The image they have of themselves, or rather the image of success that they are building that they want others to see, can take precedence over their actual relationships with other people.

Because the Western world places so much value on material success, prestige, and the drive to work hard (and often too hard), Threes are constantly rewarded for the very behavior that will hurt them in the long run. Their worst inclinations are reinforced because the wider society views them so positively. For example, working late into the night is normally praised in the corporate world, but it can lead to burnout and frayed relationships. The people around the Three who works late every night feel undervalued. Achievers need their partners to pay attention to how hard they are working but also pull them back when they are pushing themselves too hard. They need guidance to realize that what they accomplish, while important, is not the sum of their entire worth.

Common Mistypes

Similar to other types, Threes can sometimes be mistaken for one or the other of their wings. A Three with a dominant Two wing could be mistyped as a Two, as well as a Three with a dominant Four wing could be mistyped as a Four. It is essential to pay attention to the particular personality traits of both the basic type and the wings in order to decide which is which. It can sometimes be difficult to distinguish between a 3w2 and a 2w3, but a good rule of thumb is to look at their comfort level with pursuing goals and how well they are able to access their feelings. Threes are unafraid to go after what they want in life, and there is very little to hold them back. However, a 2w3 might feel internally that being ambitious is somewhat self-centered or selfish. Twos also have much more access to their emotions than a typical Three would have, or even a 3w2. This is also similar to distinguishing the 3w4 from the 4w3. Fours have much freer access to their feelings and emotions whereas Threes can suppress their emotions in order to focus on the task at hand.

Threes, Sevens, and Eights also have quite a few similarities that can make it challenging for newcomers to the Enneagram to tell them apart. All three are assertive stances that focus on the future, and they are also all very goal-oriented in some way. However, Threes are mainly focused on achieving some kind of success within their personal or professional life. Meanwhile, Sevens are drawn to the experience itself rather than the end goal of having succeeded at something. They live for the adventure instead of the end result. Eights and Threes are both characterized by their ambition and competitiveness. While Eights want to dominate and wield power in some way, they are generally uninterested in status or how others view them and their achievements. Part of the reason Threes are so motivated by success is that they want to be seen by others and admired for their success. Threes are the true status seekers over the Seven and the Eight.

Wing Personalities

Threes can have either a Two wing or a Four wing. The Charmer (3w2) is more sociable and drawn to people while The Professional (3w4) tends to have a better understanding of their emotions. They are also more likely to have a creative outlet of some kind. Twos are characterized by their desire to be loved and needed, so the 3w2 is a more extroverted version of a Two. They might be flashier than a 3w4, as well as more focused on their image and how they appear to other people. Their own personal success might be just as much for others (they want to appear successful to the outside world) as it is for themselves.

Threes love to charm others, hence their moniker of The Charmer. On the other hand, Fours are far more introverted and often have a fundamental belief that there is something different, missing, or unique about them. Paired with the basic type of Three, a 3w4 would be a more introverted version of their Charmer counterpart. The Professional is still ambitious, but they would perhaps temper their flashiness and show more caution when approaching their goals and how they undertake their endeavors. Because they have a more withdrawn, introverted wing, they may also draw back and spend more time alone than the more outgoing and gregarious Charmer.

Acceptance

Threes have the ability to completely disassociate themselves from their feelings and emotions. This is especially true when they focus themselves so intensely on a specific task or goal that is important to them. Threes are concerned with success and hard work, and they can repress their emotions and needs in order to achieve whatever goal they have set for themselves. This tendency to ignore everything and everyone around them that does not serve their immediate purpose can have a negative effect on their personal relationships. The people in their lives might feel ignored or even shunned. During conversations with their loved ones, a Three might seem distracted, thinking about all of the things they have to do in order to reach their goal.

Being an aggressive stance, Threes are very future-oriented. They tend to be relatively uninterested in the past, so they do not necessarily like discussing or rehashing what went wrong. They would be much more responsive and inclined to hear suggestions about how they can make improvements in the future, implement strategies, and achieve goals to strengthen their relationships. When Threes are too focused on their own personal goals and endeavors, they can unintentionally push those around them away or exclude them from their lives. They do not mind criticism and critique, but they respond well when it is mixed with praise and affirmation for what they are doing well. While everything Threes do needs to be affirmed, they also need to know that they are loved for who they are rather than merely for what they succeed at doing.

FOUR: The Individualist

Levels of Health and Development

When Fours are doing well, they take on the more positive, grounded, and focused traits of the One. Fours are a withdrawing stance, and they are often far more concentrated on the past than the present or future. In contrast, Ones are a dependent stance intent on living in the present moment. When Fours move into health, they are also able to integrate into being in the present moment, living life as it comes rather than daydreaming about the past or ruminating on feelings and regrets. Healthy Fours are also able to set more emotional boundaries due to the One's more black-and-white style of thinking. They are less controlled by the ferocity of their emotions and are able to rein them in with more ease. This also means that healthy Fours are able to complete tasks and reach goals regardless of how they might be feeling at the moment. Ones follow through on what they say they will do, and Fours take on this quality in their best moments.

On the other hand, when Fours move into the unhealthier regions of their personality, they take on the traits of another member of the Feeling Center, the Two. Unhealthy Twos are often people-pleasing, possessive of others, and manipulative in order to get what they want: affection and affirmation. Fours in stress believe themselves to be lacking in some way, defective, or undesirable. At their unhealthiest, they can even view themselves as perpetual victims in search of someone or something to save them from their own darkest tendencies.

Healthy: Levels 1, 2, and 3

- Healthy Fours are brimming with inspiration and creativity, and their art is often very personal and self-reflective. They are aware of their emotions, and they are also aware of how their emotions can make other people feel. These Fours are very intuitive, devoted to honesty and authenticity, and in pursuit of both self-knowledge and self-awareness.

Average: Levels 4, 5, and 6

- Average Fours are imaginative and artistic, but they can also become overly sensitive and absorbed within their own emotions. They take almost everything personally, and they can become self-conscious of themselves and everything they do. They might feel that nothing they put effort in lives up to the expections of both themselves and others. To deal with these feelings, these Fours might disappear into the fantasies and daydreams they create in their minds.

Unhealthy: Levels 7, 8, and 9

- Unhealthy Fours can become self-destructive due to disappointment with themselves and the dreams or endeavors that they have attempted to accomplish. At their unhealthiest, they can begin feeling a sense of contempt and even hatred toward themselves. These Fours can also develop problems with drugs or alcohol in their attempts to self-medicate.

Communication

Fours are the most emotionally expressive type on the Enneagram. At every level of health, they are in touch with their emotions and how they are feeling. This can be a bit overwhelming for some of the other numbers that are not so in emotionally aware. Fours are especially inclined toward darkness and melancholy, which most other types are not so comfortable with. Fours are also drawn toward poetry, art, beauty, and embellished language to fully express how they feel. They love to paint with words, either their own or those of other artists from the past, to convey the depth of how they feel and what they want you to know about them. Fours are often more comfortable with writing out their sentiments than speaking them aloud, and their writings can get rather lengthy. They communicate both their positive and negative emotions through a dramatic medium of some kind.

When Fours are angry or upset, which can be often, they can either completely withdraw and give an extreme cold shoulder treatment or alternatively, let out their anger in a wild stream of emotion. While Fours' feelings might seem over the top to others, it is essential that they be validated rather than ignored or dismissed. It is also important not to tell them to cheer up or put on a smile since Fours are accustomed to living with the somber and melancholy. To them, having these feelings does not mean that they are depressed or even sad.

Intimacy

To many other types on the Enneagram, Fours can often come across as sad or depressed. However, this is not the case. More than any other type, Fours are able to sit with their grief, sorrow, or pensive, melancholic thoughts. They do not need to happy all the time, nor do they want to be. One problem with this, mostly for the other numbers, is that they often withdraw from the Four because they are simply not able to hold onto such dark emotions without feeling overwhelmed themselves. The Four then feels that they are too dramatic, too dark, or just too much for others to handle. This can push them to seal themselves off further from other people and feel that there is something intrinsically wrong with them.

It can also make it more difficult for the Four to open up to others in the future because they are so fearful of sharing the depths of the emotions they feel within themselves. They don't want to overwhelm anyone else and drive them away with their intensity. Fours need someone who can handle the full range of their emotions without being turned off or turned away by them. They also need someone who understands that just because they aren't happy, it doesn't mean that they are sad.

Common Mistypes

As with other types, Fours can be mistaken for their more dominant wing. This is more likely with the Five than the Four since both Fours and Fives are withdrawing stances and can be mistaken for each other. However, it is generally more difficult to distinguish between the 4w5 and the 5w4 than it is to judge between the Four and the Five themselves. Both are withdrawn, introverted, and value independence. However, Fours are far more in touch with their feelings than even a Five with a dominant Four wing would be. Being in the Thinking Center, a Five lives much more within their head and thoughts than in their emotions.

Fours can sometimes be confused with Sixes, although it is mostly Sixes who think they are Fours rather than the other way around. This happens most often when a Six, whose type does tend to be more pessimistic than most, identifies with the Four traits in stress. However, Fours are usually stressed by disappointment with themselves rather than difficulties with an outside entity (such as an authority figure) as with the Six. Sixes are also usually quite sociable and enjoy spending time with other people and relating to them in some way.

On the other hand, Fours are generally quite happy to be left alone. They don't necessarily need to spend a lot of time with other people and are perfectly content with what is going on in their own minds. Nines can also often mistake themselves for Fours. This happens especially with those Nines that have an artistic inclination of some kind. However, one telltale difference between the artistry of the two types is that Fours tend to put a lot of their own experience into their work. In contrast, an artistic Nine will be drawn to mythological motifs where an image or archetype stands for something else that all of humankind could perhaps relate to in some way. Another difference between the two types is that Nines disassociate themselves from their emotions while Fours wallow in their feelings and only withdraw from what has hurt them rather than from the pain itself.

Wing Personalities

Fours can have either a dominant Three wing or Five wing. The Aristocrat (4w3) is firmly placed, with both their basic type and their dominant wing, in the Feeling Center. They are more driven and focused than their 4w5 counterparts, and they are able to follow through better and with more success when it comes to their ambitions. And having a Three wing means that they might have grand ambitions they want to achieve. The 4w3 also tends to have a more traditional work ethic than other Fours, and they can lean into their Three wing's strengths of being more social and extroverted than a typical Four might otherwise be. The Bohemian (4w5) has a dominant wing in the Thinking Center, so they are able to lean into those Five strengths of research, knowledge, and intellectualism.

Fives are the most isolated and reserved of all the Enneagram types, so the 4w5 is usually more introverted and withdrawn than their counterparts with a Three wing. Both Fours tend to have some inclination toward creativity, whether they are actually artists by trade or hobby. The Bohemian is often very eclectic, isolated, and independent while The Aristocrat is more aware of what is expected of them in order to succeed and sell themselves and their creative endeavors.

Acceptance

Fours are very private individuals. They are probably the most private type on the Enneagram apart from the Five. While they feel their emotions strongly, they can also frequently second-guess them. Because how they feel is so complex - a Four might feel the sadness or nostalgia combined with the happiness of hope tinged with the sorrow of loss all in the same couple of minutes - they often prefer to keep their feelings to themselves since others have so often been unable to comprehend them. The Individualist is comfortable with darker thoughts and melancholy, and they often do not want to be told to cheer up or look happier. In reality, they are neither depressed nor sad. They want (and need) to feel and express the entire range of their emotions. They also need to be accepted and validated, emotions and all, by the people in their lives. This is especially true when they have opened up to someone and feel comfortable enough to show their vulnerability.

Due to their wide array of emotions, Fours often need quite a bit of time to process how they are feeling and how they want to approach a relationship or situation. It is normal for Fours to withdrawn for a time, and this can even be a frequent occurrence. Their feelings, emotions, sense of vulnerability, and need for time spent alone should always be accepted with understanding.

FIVE: The Investigator

Levels of Health and Development

When Fives are at their best, they take on the more positive traits of the Eight. They become more confident, self-assured, and are able to show more extroversion and comfort with social interactions. These Fives are able to get in touch with their emotions and rely less on their purely analytical skills. They are able to get out of their head and back into their body. More so than the other two Thinking Center types, the Six and the Seven, Fives live predominantly in their heads using their keen intellects and powers of analysis to experience the world from a safe distance. As a withdrawing stance type, Fives are "doing repressed." But as they integrate toward Eight, one of the types in the Instinctive or Body Center, Fives are able to more fully inhabit their physicality. Integrating Fives are able to more easily take action rather than simply thinking about it.

Conversely, Fives that are in the process of disintegrating into stress begin to show the more negative aspects of the type Seven. Their actions can become erratic and disorganized. Their normal ability to keep calm and ordered evaporates into distraction and short attention spans. They search for anything that will distract them from whatever it is that might be worrying them, and this can include substance abuse. Under normal circumstances, Fives are the most withdrawn and measured of all the Enneagram types. Under stress, however, they can become dangerously impulsive and don't always think before taking action. Disintegrating Fives leave their intellectual capacity for thorough thinking and instead think almost nothing.

Healthy: Levels 1, 2, and 3

- Healthy Fives have an incredible capacity for understanding the world, comprehending complex ideas in their entirety, and keeping their minds open to understand new things. They are drawn to the acquisition of new knowledge and mastering their wide array of interests. These Fives are extremely independent and are comfortable with their perceived eccentricities.

Average: Levels 4, 5, and 6

- Average Fives begin to concern themselves more and more with acquiring vast amounts of knowledge in order to safeguard themselves from perceived insecurities. They can also start withdrawing for expensive periods of time and creating worlds within their minds that are safe for them to inhabit. As they descend further, Fives can begin to have a cynical outlook on life.

Unhealthy: Levels 7, 8, and 9

- Unhealthy Fives can become recluses, hiding themselves from the world and developing a dark and even nihilistic worldview. These Fives can even become aggressive when forced into social interactions. Like the Four, they may also try to self-medicate with drugs, alcohol, or anything else that promises to relieve their stress and anxiety.

Communication

Fives are the most introverted and withdrawn of all the types on the Enneagram, even among the three withdrawing stance types. They spend a huge amount of time alone devoted to whichever endeavor best helps them pursue their intellectual interests. Because they spend so much time on their own, Fives sometimes find it difficult to communicate with other people in effective ways. They might simply not have had as much practice as the other types. This is especially true when heightened emotions are involved since Fives also do not normally associate themselves very closely with how they feel. They often prefer to stand back and observe activities or events rather than actually participate in them. However, Fives excel at communication when it comes to explaining something that they have researched or spent time understanding clearly and thoroughly.

In some respects, Fives are the stereotypical university professor: intellectually brilliant but detached from their feelings and how they can relate to people on an emotional level. Their style of speaking is often quite formal, and they like to use technical, unbiased, and precise language to formulate their ideas and get their point across. In altercations, Fives in particular can become quite passive aggressive. This is true when they are angry or even just annoyed. It is important that Fives be given a space to express themselves, and for those around them not to shine a spotlight on them when they show up to voice their opinions since they generally do not like to be the center of attention.

Intimacy

Fives tend to be very heady and intellectual types. They enjoy thinking and are often lost in their own thoughts, analyzing one thing or another. They do not like the spotlight, so asking them an open-ended question like, "What are you thinking about?" can feel like an interrogation to them. Asking a more pointed question like, "What do you think about *this*?" is much more in line with what they might feel up to contributing. Otherwise they could feel put on the spot, and they do not enjoy being the center of attention. It also gives the Five a chance to offer some of their expertise on a topic which they probably know a good deal about.

Although they hide them, Fives do have feelings and emotions. They tend to suppress them because they don't often feel comfortable so overtly expressing how they feel. It is important not to draw attention to the Five when they do display some of their emotions. Being very private individuals, they would probably not appreciate the drama of being made the object of others' attention in this way. Many Fives are so private and reserved that they do not even wish to participate in things like class discussions, conference calls, or meetings. This does not mean that they are not paying attention, taking notes, or filing information away for future use. Fives prefer observing to participating, although as they move toward health, they are more comfortable with getting out of their head and into experiencing life in new ways. Fives need someone who understands that silence is synonymous with neither agreement nor anger, and who can understand and support their need for time spent alone while also pushing them gently toward moving outside their comfort zone.

Common Mistypes

Fives can sometimes be mistaken for a Four because both types tend to be very introverted, especially when certain wings and instinctual variants are taken into account. Both Fours and Fives are withdrawing stances, which tend to be very introverted and can easily isolate themselves for long periods of time. Fives are usually the more isolated of the two. The 5w4 and the 4w5 are also often very difficult to differentiate because they can have so many similarities. Fives tend to be more focused on analysis - data, science and information, while Fours are drawn more to free flowing creativity. Whichever of those two is stronger is likely to be the basic type while the weaker one is the dominant wing. Sixes can also sometimes mistype themselves as Fives, although the opposite is less likely.

Both types are located in the Thinking Center, and both are focused on analysis. Sixes, however, are usually more practical and research specific topics that can help them feel safe and secure. Nines can also mistype themselves as Fives. Just as with the Four, both types are withdrawing stances. They both spend a lot of time alone, but their motives are different. Apart from the Five's two possible wings (Four and Six), it is far more common for other types to mistype themselves as Fives than it is for a Five to misidentify themselves as another type.

Wing Personalities

Fives can have either a Four wing or a Six wing. The Iconoclast (5w4) takes on more elements of the Four personality when The Individualist is their more dominant wing. They seek knowledge more for the sake of having and forming a unique identity or expressing their emotions and ideas through intellectual pursuits. They can also be much more drawn to pleasing aesthetics and melancholy, than their 5w6 counterparts. When Fives have a more developed Four wing, they tend to be more in touch with their feelings and creativity than a typical Five would be. Since both their basic number and their dominant wing are withdrawing stances that tend to be more introverted, Iconoclasts are perhaps the most reserved and isolated of all the Enneagram types.

On the other hand, The Problem Solver (5w6) pursues knowledge not for expression or identity but rather for safety and security. These Fives are much more analytical and data-oriented than their 5w4 counterparts. They are more influenced by their need to protect themselves and those in their lives than for a more nebulous love of knowledge such as The Iconoclast is often after. While Problem Solvers are also introverts, they tend to be less so than those Fives with a Four wing. They still prefer to be alone, but they do genuinely enjoy the company of others from time to time and seek them out when they are in need of human contact. However, they can also disassociate themselves from their emotions and rely solely on their formidable skills of logic and analysis to make decisions.

Acceptance

Fives are the most introverted and withdrawn of all the Enneagram types, and they often isolate themselves from other people when they need their time alone. And they do need a lot of alone time. Fives have a difficult time with their energy levels, and they frequently feel like they do not have enough of it to complete all of the tasks and goals they have set for themselves. Fives are devoted to accumulating as much knowledge, understanding, and information as possible to help them stave off their fear of being inadequate or unprepared for life, but this also means that they spend huge amounts of time alone reading, researching, and thinking through what they have learned. Most Fives are also not very in touch with their feelings and emotions, so they may not notice when they are inadvertently giving the cold shoulder to their loved ones. Fives need a partner who can pull them out of their isolation from time to time, but they also need someone who will give them enough time and space to continue pursuing the things that they love on their own.

SIX: The Loyalist

Levels of Health and Development

When Sixes are integrating and moving forward into the healthier regions of their personality, they take on the more positive aspects of type Nine. They become more relaxed and at ease, and they are able to listen much less to the constant stream of worries that normally runs through their minds. Nines are part of the Instinctive Center, and when Sixes integrate toward this type, they are able to get out of their heads so much and listen more to their inner gut reactions. These integrating Sixes are also able to become more independent in their daily lives. Sixes normally need affirmation from an outside force or entity. This usually takes the form of an authority figure or system of some kind. As they become healthier, they are able to listen to themselves and their own interior authority more.

When Sixes disintegrate, they move toward type Three. Unhealthy Threes are characterized by their tendency toward brutal competition and their high opinions of themselves. Sixes can take on some of these qualities as well when they are feeling stressed. Unhealthy Sixes can become workaholics, obsessing over every small detail of their own work, lives, or relationships in an attempt to control and micromanage both themselves and others. This has the effect of giving them some of the sense of security that they are searching for.

Healthy: Levels 1, 2, and 3

- Healthy Sixes are able to trust themselves as well as others to a deeper level. They are also able to become more independent rather than only relying upon an authority outside of their own experiences. These Sixes build relationships, invest in their communities, and cooperate with others to establish a safe, secure, and stable environment.

Average: Levels 4, 5, and 6

- Average Sixes begin turning to structure and order to ensure their sense of safety and security. They place their trust in authority figures or organizations. These Sixes tend to play out all of the possible worst-case scenarios in their minds and imagine ways to deal with them. As they descend further, they may blame others for their problems. They may also become passive-aggressive and sarcastic in their dealings with other people.

Unhealthy: Levels 7, 8, and 9

- Unhealthy Sixes become not just passive-aggressive, but actually aggressive. They can take on an us-vs-them mentality, seeing everyone who is not them or on their side as someone who is against them. These Sixes might turn to violence, conspiracy theories, and extremism. They can act irrationally to the point of being self-destructive.

Communication

Sixes like to have a lot of information at their disposal. If they don't think they have enough, they can begin to overthink and are not at ease with whatever situation they might find themselves in. Sixes also tend to ask a lot of questions if they feel short on information. They want to understand everything because they are then able to plan more thoroughly for any possible situation that might arise. They are usually not trying to challenge anyone or make anyone feel inept or insufficient by asking many questions; the Six truly needs this information for their own purposes. Not having enough information can make them feel more pressure, anxiety, and insecurity. Sixes do not like to be surprised by anything they did not expect, so they prefer to have as many pieces of information as possible to maintain the predictable routines with which they are comfortable. When Sixes feel comfortable enough with their friend or partner, they may begin to open up and share things most likely to put pressure and anxiety on them. However, it is important to remember that they are not asking their partner to fix these issues. They are rather only in need of acknowledgment of their weaknesses and perhaps looking for help in working through them.

Intimacy

As The Loyalist, Sixes are extremely loyal individuals to those they love and care about. This stems from their inner fear of being left behind, taken for granted, or abandoned. They are fearful of being left on their own, and so they compensate by playing out every scenario imaginable in their head and how to counteract it. Their insecurities often define their relationships, and they are frequently unwilling to take risks or put themselves on the line in any way. Sixes do not like to feel vulnerable in this regard.

It is important to reinforce a personal connection with the Six so that they know on an intimate level that they can rely on their partner's continuing presence in their lives. They also need a partner who will listen without judgment to their fears and anxieties, no matter how illogical they might sound to someone who is not a Six. Loyalists do not often listen to or rely on their own inner voice, so it is important for their partners to help them begin looking to themselves as well as the authority figures and organizations that they often put trust in.

Common Mistypes

As with most other types, Sixes can misidentify as one or the other of their wings. If one wing is particularly strong, a Six might have trouble distinguishing themselves between their dominant type and either their Five or Seven wing. A good way to tell the difference between a 6w7 and a 7w6 is to look at how they view planning. The 7w6 tends to enjoy planning things even if they might end up veering off of their own schedules in the moment. Meanwhile, the 6w7 does not enjoy drawing up plans in the same way. They might be more spontaneous than the Seven with a dominant Six wing. For those with a Five wing, it is more common for Sixes to misidentify as Fives than for Fives to misidentify as Sixes, although it is still not the most common of mistypes for a Six to make. That would be the difficulties telling apart the Six and the Nine. Both Sixes and Nines prefer stability and security as well as for things to stay the same with as few surprises as possible.

Both types are also relationship-oriented, whether it be with family or friends. One way to tell them apart is to look at how they react to stress. Nines value peace and tranquility, so they are more able to slog through difficulties without showing much emotion whereas the Six is more prone to showing their anxiety and any defensive postures that they may take on to protect themselves.

Wing Personalities

Sixes can have either a dominant Five wing or Seven wing. The Defender (6w5) tends to be more reserved and self-reliant than their counterparts with a Seven wing. They show more independence in their relationships and activities, and they are much more introverted than the 6w7. Both Fives and Sixes are located in the Thinking Center, and both types are driven by fear is some way. For the 6w5, the fears of each type serve to reinforce each other. Sixes are afraid of fear itself, and they are often suspicious of other people's motivations and intentions. They can become very anxious about what other types would consider insignificant difficulties.

Fives can also manifest anxiety when they do not know something on an intellectual level. A 6w5 can be doubly anxious and can often withdraw from people and situations. On the other hand, The Buddy (6w7) is much more sociable and outdoing due to their dominant Seven wing. Sevens are some of the most lively and extroverted people on the Enneagram. They are often willing to do or try anything, and their only true fears are of the more melancholic or upsetting experiences in life. The 6w7 tends to be much more optimistic than their 6w5 counterpart. They are more able to give into their spontaneity and love of the new and unknown. The strength of this wing counterbalances the anxiety of their basic type.

Acceptance

Sixes are characterized by their need for a safe and secure environment. They tend to dislike surprises, even good ones, and they appreciate structure that can be relied upon. Because they do not want to be surprised with anything that departs from their established routines, Sixes can become suspicious and wary of their surroundings and even the people in their lives. Due to this tendency, Sixes' innate sense of wariness needs to be accepted by their partners and communication should remain very open and direct. They can often question why people - even those in close relationships with them - are acting in a particular way. Sixes often expect the worst and plan for even worse than that. They want to protect their environment and the people they love. This is where their sense of wariness comes from. It is advisable to be extremely transparent with a Six about how you feel, what you are doing, and why you are doing it. Sixes do not want to be taken aback or caught off guard by anything. If they are confronted with anything unwanted or unexpected, it can take a long time to put them at ease and regain their trust.

SEVEN: The Enthusiast

Levels of Health and Development

When Sevens begin integrating into health, they move towards type Five. They are able to slow down more and become more introspective rather than always being focused on achieving or experiencing the next great thing they have come across or want to mark off their bucket list. Instead of filling their schedules with more and more activities to entertain themselves, they stop and savor the small moments and create a space where they can slow down and enjoy life on a smaller scale with the people they love. These healthy Sevens are able to relax on a deeper level since they do not feel the need to constantly be on the go.

Alternatively, Sevens move toward Ones when they are disintegrating into stress. They take on the more negative aspects of The Perfectionist as well as their excessively ordered tendencies. These unhealthy Sevens become more critical and demanding in their requirements for perfection, order, and being correct. Such a disintegrating Seven might nitpick or pass harsh judgment that they would normally not bother with carding about so much, if at all. Sevens in the lower regions of their personality are far more rigid and judgmental, and they can even show tendencies toward controlling others that an average or healthy Seven would not show.

Healthy: Levels 1, 2, and 3

- Healthy Sevens are able to construct a sense of thankfulness for what they do have - experiences, possessions, and so on - rather than constantly being on the search for more of the same to accumulate. They have developed gratitude rather than greed. While these Sevens are still extremely extroverted, spontaneous, and enthusiastic, they are also more practical and have honed their ability to focus on achieving their goals rather than running to the next thing when difficulties arise.

Average: Levels 4, 5, and 6

- Average Sevens want to maintain a wide array of options at their disposal. They do not want to be limited in any way. They can begin to lose focus when what they are working on becomes difficult or less enjoyable, and they are unable to see it through to completion. These Sevens are constantly on the move, always doing and rarely resting or savoring the moment. As they descend further, they can become more selfish and self-centered.

Unhealthy: Levels 7, 8, and 9

- Unhealthy Sevens are anxious, and they look for anything with the ability to put them at ease. They become impulsive, erratic, and can even lose control of themselves. At their lowest, they can become exhausted as a result of being unable to rest or take time for themselves to relax. There is also the risk of substance abuse and addiction at this level of health.

Communication

Sevens possess fast-moving minds. They are always jumping from one idea or plan to the next. To other types, Sevens can appear frenzied with no rhyme or reason to their apparently random thoughts. But the topics make sense in the mind of the Seven, and there is a method to their perceived madness. They are usually quick to share their thoughts, opinions, ideas, and suggestions, and they are often also quick to say yes to most things. It can be quite hurtful to a Seven if their seemingly jumbled thoughts and ideas are dismissed or disregarded without any serious consideration or acknowledgement. They will not often show or say they have been offended or hurt, but Sevens can be just as sensitive as other types on the Enneagram. Sevens can also be misread as rude or shallow because they often interrupt others in their excitement or move from topic to topic with such speed. While Sevens do need to learn how to slow down and give space to others who are not as exuberant or unreserved in their personal style, accusing them of not listening or of being rude and unfocused is not a constructive method.

Intimacy

More than any other type on the Enneagram, Sevens are free spirits. They are bright, lively, and enigmatic individuals always on the lookout for the next great thing to experience or adventure to undertake. Sevens are rarely known for being homebodies, nor are they particularly interested in relaxing for lengthy periods of time. They are also often repelled by the heavier experiences or conversations that are a part of any relationship, and they will almost certainly avoid such things. In this respect, they are the exact opposite of the Four. Fours can find the enjoyment within the melancholy of sadness, pain, and anger. Sevens run from all of those things, not wanting to experience any of them. This is important for a Seven's partner to know and understand. More difficult conversations or experiences are going to inevitably be a part of any relationship, but with a Seven, it is important to keep those conversations or experiences as short as possible. Sevens may also need time to process these more negative experiences and melancholic emotions.

Common Mistypes

As with other types on the Enneagram, Sevens may misidentify themselves as one of their dominant wings, either the Six or the Eight. But they can also mistype themselves as a number of other types. A Seven might mistype themselves as a One if they are particularly low in their level of health. They may have become overly rigid and perfectionistic, much like unhealthy Ones. As Sevens move further into their healthier regions, this rigidity and excessive need for order will fall away to reveal the more enthusiastic and carefree personality of a typical Seven. Twos and Sevens can also sometimes be mistaken for each other since they are both so warm and loving to those around them.

Both types are not afraid to display their emotions, although the Seven does tend to be more dramatic than the Two in this respect. While both types are also interested in people and enjoy spending time with others, Twos tend to be much more devoted to interpersonal communication than the Seven. On the other hand, Sevens do not normally involve themselves in others' lives unless they have been invited, while Twos are more likely to invite themselves in.

Lastly, Sevens and Threes can also come across as similar in many respects. They are both aggressive stance types that move against people and are oriented toward the future. They both spend their time in aggressive pursuit of what is important to them. However, Sevens pursue enriching experiences (and sometimes possessions) as a way of accumulating a rich history of sensations. Threes pursue success, as well as, wealth and fame for their own image and self-importance. Sevens wants stimulation while Threes prefer status.

Wing Personalities

Sevens can have either a dominant Six wing or Eight wing. The Entertainer (7w6) is a curious mix of introvert and extrovert qualities. Sevens are one of the most extroverted types on the Enneagram, along with the Three and the Eight, and they have the possibility of being paired with a Six wing which is often more introverted. Because Sixes are nicknamed The Loyalist, a Seven with a Six wing is more likely to have a more tempered relationship with commitment and stability than a Seven with a weaker Six wing. Sevens are afraid of commitment, but Sixes are devoted to it. Since both their basic number and their dominant wing are located in the Thinking Center, they have a stronger connection to the underlying fear and anxiety that motivates them.

On the other hand, The Realist (7w8) combines two very extroverted types. Both the Seven (The Enthusiast) and the Eight (The Challenger) are driven, extroverted, and unwaveringly unapologetic when it comes to the force of their personalities. Since the Eight is located within the Instinctive Center, Realists have more access to their gut reactions and anger than that of the 7w6 whose types are both centered only in the Thinking Center. The 7w8 is more energetic, passionate, and decisive than their 7w6 counterparts.

Acceptance

Sevens are spontaneous, adventurous, and are able to achieve a near constant level of activity. They have a persistently optimistic energy about them. Of all the types on the Enneagram, they are the most fun-loving and lighthearted. However, this is often all that they search for or allow themselves to experience in life. They have a tendency to run from anything that might prove to be negative or unenjoyable, including things they know they need to do, feel, or accomplish. Sevens are oriented around the future rather than the past or the present, so they are always chasing after the next great thing or experience. Being held back or held down in some way can set a Seven off and make them feel trapped or even confined by a sense of claustrophobia. This is the reason that Sevens sometimes struggle with long-term commitments and even long-term relationships. They are afraid of being trapped by something that they may not want in the future. Sevens do not want to be limited in what they are free and able to experience in life. A Seven's partner needs to understand this fear of missing out on life experiences, as well as their inability or unwillingness to feel emotions of the darker, more melancholic variety. A Seven needs their partner to help them slow down and savor life as well as draw closer to the emotions that they have inside of them but have spent their lives ignoring.

EIGHT: The Challenger

Levels of Health and Development

As Eights integrate into health, they move toward type Two. Eights are naturally quite forceful personalities, and they are the most aggressive type on the Enneagram. They are normally not very concerned with how other people feel. This is not because they don't care about others but because it simply does not initially occur to them. As Eights move toward health, they take on the characteristics of the Two. They begin to look to others' perspectives and listen to what the people around them are thinking and feeling. Healthy Eights can allow themselves to feel a sense of vulnerability that unhealthy Eights are incapable of giving into.

When Eights descend into the unhealthier regions of their personality, they disintegrate towards type Five. Although naturally extroverted, they begin behaving more like an introvert. They remove themselves from their lives and withdraw into isolation. While remaining out of touch with their emotions or self-expression, unhealthy Eights can become even more detached and unable to display how they feel. Unhealthy Eights can also begin to view everyone and everything around them as a threat that must be dealt with. They can become rigid and inflexible in how they take in their environment, lashing out at anyone who dares to cross them.

Healthy: Levels 1, 2, and 3

- Healthy Eights still show a lot of personal strength and self-confidence, but it has been tempered with self-restraint. They are also much more comfortable with vulnerability, and they often develop a gentleness that listens to and values other people. Healthy Eights are very resourceful, and they can make excellent leaders, especially during great difficulties.

Average: Levels 4, 5, and 6

- Average Eights are unapologetic individualists, and they work incredibly hard to achieve their goals. They value independence in both themselves and others. As they continue descending into stress, Eights can become more self-centered and egocentric. They can even resort to using threats and intimidation to get what they want or bully others to get their way.

Unhealthy: Levels 7, 8, and 9

- Unhealthy Eights are reckless, adversarial, and defiant. These Eights can have a tendency to resort to criminal activity or even violence when they have descended so deeply into their own stress and the darker regions of their personality. They often build up images of themselves and their own power that are not based in reality. If they feel someone has crossed them, they will likely try to take revenge in some way.

Communication

Eights are very straightforward people. They do not beat around the bush. They get right to the point. This can feel overly direct and even aggressive to some of the other types on the Enneagram, but the Eight does not necessarily mean to come across this way. It is often the same with their volume control. Eights are often loud, or at least louder than the rest of the people around them. Most of the time, they do not necessarily mean to come across in such an exuberant and domineering way. Eights also have the tendency to come across as strong, forceful, brusque, and unemotional. While they are often all of these things, they can also take on their opposite characteristics even though they may try to hide it. Eights hide their vulnerabilities because they are afraid of opening themselves up to being controlled by others. Eights can feel just as deeply as the other types, but they are well versed in covering up their more vulnerable side unless they feel very safe exposing it. Eights appreciate honesty. They view anything less as being fake and even manipulative. This includes flattery. Eights would rather have a confrontation based on honest feelings than a friendly yet superficial conversation.

Intimacy

Eights are all about protection. They look out for themselves, and they look out for the people around them whom they care about. Those are their two most important things in life. Eights will do anything and everything to achieve these twin goals, and they are unafraid of being aggressive, confrontational, threatening, and intimidating. Eights are perhaps the most physical of all the types on the Enneagram, and many of them take part in sports. They often have a physicality about them that they can use to their advantage when protecting both themselves and the people they love when necessary. Eights are also drawn to strength, and they run from vulnerability.

When interacting with an Eight, it is also important to always be honest and stand your ground in any conflict. Eights do not necessarily perceive conflict as a negative thing, so they would likely be inclined to respect those who stand up to them rather than find it offensive. They can also view flattery as manipulative and superficial. Eights need a partner who is not overpowered by their own personality. They also need someone with who can provide them with a safe place to feel vulnerable.

Common Mistypes

Eights can sometimes confuse themselves with one of the other two aggressive stance types: the Three and the Seven. But there are some telling differences between them. Eights and Threes are both extremely competitive, but Eights are not really driven by material success or status. They do not care nearly so much as Threes about how others view them and their social status. Threes compare themselves to others a lot, perhaps more than any other number on the Enneagram, whereas Eights seldom do. It is also more common for Threes to misidentify themselves as Eights rather than the other way around. The other aggressive stance, the Seven, can also sometimes be confused with the Eight. A key difference between them is that Sevens are in search of a variety of experiences while Eights are in search of experiences with intensity. Sevens want to try everything they can possibly cram into their lives, but Eights are more interested in how deep their experiences can take them.

Twos can also sometimes mistake themselves for Eights when they are disintegrating into stress. Eight is the Two's stress point. This tendency is especially true for male Twos who, for cultural reasons, are often pressured to be more forceful and domineering. However, it is less likely for an Eight to mistype themselves as a Two. Even when Eights are integrating towards a Two, it is not common for Eights to think that they are actually Twos. While Twos may attempt to control others, they would not try to overpower others. An Eight would be far more likely to use force or aggression than mere manipulation.

Wing Personalities

Eights can have either a dominant Seven wing or Nine wing. The Maverick (8w7) can be quite ambitious and aggressive. Both the basic type and dominant wing are aggressive stance types, so The Maverick tends to be very extroverted. Eights are already a very impulsive type, but Sevens can be as well. They often have poor impulse control and will often take actions that they otherwise know they shouldn't. The goals that this type sets for themselves are usually met. The 8w7 is very resourceful and thus able to reach their goals more easily than the 8w9. In contrast, The Bear (8w9) is more laid back and easygoing due to their dominant Nine wing. Nines are known as The Peacemaker, so this stronger wing serves to balance out the more aggressive characteristics of the Eight. They are able to lean into the Nine wing when necessary to come across as more gentle, relaxed, and diplomatic. While an 8w7 might run to each and every conflict that crosses their path, an 8w9 is more likely to pick and choose which ones are important to them. They are more aware that not every battle is worth fighting with their limited internal resources.

Acceptance

Eights are the most aggressive of all the types on the Enneagram. This does not mean that they are vicious or unfriendly in any way. They just have a tendency to be forceful, demanding, and straightforward in their communication style. It is important for Eights to be accepted for who they are in this regard. They should be allowed to embrace the intensity of their personalities while simultaneously be provided with a safe space to be vulnerable without feeling like they are being taken advantage of. Eights fear being controlled by others, so they often turn to controlling others as a way to ward off any threat. When their partners have provided them with acceptance and a safe environment to be themselves, Eights will often become more playful and vulnerable. They become open to the acceptance of other people, and become less drawn to the need for conflict that characterises them during less healthy levels.

NINE: The Peacemaker

Levels of Health and Development

Nines in health move toward type Three. They become energetic, focused, and driven. These healthy Nines are able to see the significance they can bring into the world, and they push themselves forward to actively contribute to their relationships, professional projects, and communities. They become more confident and show much less fear and insecurity about taking up space in the world. Healthy Nines are also more able to set goals and implement steps to attain them. Average to unhealthy Nines struggle with being proactive, but Nines moving toward health are able to take on the positive attributes of the Three in order to become more proactive in their daily lives. Alternatively, Nines move toward Six when they become stressed and begin to disintegrate. Unhealthy Nines can become anxious, stressed, and are often frozen in fear and find themselves unable to take action. Nines are normally averse to any kind of emotional display, especially ones that are angry or upset. After suppressing their emotions for too long, unhealthy Nines can sometimes explode in anger.

Healthy: Levels 1, 2, and 3

- Healthy Nines have become secure in their own identity and show little of the self-consciousness that can define average or unhealthy Nines. These healthy Nines can often exude a calming presence that puts others at ease. They can also allow themselves to move into action in order to achieve their goals since they no longer stick to the lethargy that had characterized them in their lower levels of health.

Average: Levels 4, 5, and 6

- Average Nines live by the mantra of "go along to get along." They fear conflict, so they are untruthful about what it is they really want from others or even from themselves. These Nines can begin to procrastinate as they approach their more unhealthy levels, which in turn pushes them away from others and makes them feel even more isolated.

Unhealthy: Levels 7, 8, and 9

- Unhealthy Nines have become completely incapable of handling conflict or disagreement. They repress their darker emotions, most notably anger, and are unable to express themselves with confidence. Unhealthy Nines they can often feel numb to both themselves and those around them.

Communication

Nines avoid confrontation and conflict at almost any cost, so they often do not fully express themselves. They do not want to risk any kind of misunderstanding or altercation. If their ideas are dismissed, or if they are talked over or ignored, Nines can seal themselves off from the conversation. Many times, they will not fight for themselves unless they are pushed to do so. Nines feel compelled to voice their opinions, however, they might not be aware of how to speak up and make their ideas known to another person or group of people.

While Nines are not extremely talkative, they do need space to open up and talk through their perspective when they do wish to make a point or share their opinion. They also like to be asked questions. Other types might think that Nines are aloof or uninterested in the conversation, but this is normally not the case. Nines need more time to think through their ideas and formulate their thoughts into coherent sentences. If they are asked a pointed question, this makes it much easier for the Nine to put their ideas into words.

Intimacy

Nines are known as The Peacemaker. They value peace and tranquility, and they will do almost anything they can to avoid arguments or drama. Much of this is subconscious on their part. They will often merge with the people around them, agreeing or appearing to agree in order to avoid a confrontation. Nines come across as calm, measured, polite, and very aware of their surroundings. This includes the people with whom they are interacting. Nines are also quite reserved individuals, so it can take a lot of prodding to get a Nine to share their true feelings and opinions. They need to feel safe in an environment or among people who will not challenge them directly or aggressively. They do not like conflict or arguments of any kind and will go to almost any length to avoid them, even going so far as to suppress themselves. But this oftentimes will make the Nine feel resentful that they cannot express themselves truly and authentically.

Common Mistypes

Of all the types, Nines have the most difficulty in figuring out their type because they have a less defined sense of self than any of the other numbers on the Enneagram. They have spent their lives merging with others so as to avoid conflict, and now they find that they have less of a sense of individuality than the other types. This is one reason why the Nine sits atop the Enneagram looking down at all of the others, absorbing their qualities. Nines can sometimes mistake themselves for their more dominant wing. This is much more common with a One than it is with an Eight.

Eights are far more aggressive than either Nines or Ones, and they can both fall asleep to their anger for different reasons. Nines can also frequently think that they are Twos. This is especially common with both average Nines, as well as, women who are often socially conditioned to take on the traits of Twos. It is much less common for Twos to think that they are Nines. One way to tell the difference between a Nine and a Two is in how they view their affection for others. Twos almost always have a hidden motive when they express their feelings and affection; they want to feel loved, accepted, or needed in return. Nines are more selfless in this respect. They do not need the emotional reinforcement of reciprocal love in the same way as the Two. Nines focus less on themselves than a Two would when it comes to interpersonal relationships and showing affection.

One of the more common mistypings is between the Nine and the Four. Both are withdrawing stance types, and both are very introverted. Nines and Fours are also strongly creative, but it is more common for Nines to think that they are Fours rather than the other way around. One method of telling the difference between artistic Nines and Fours is how personal their art is. Fours express themselves very personally in their projects while Nines rely more on mythology, archetypes, or subconscious motifs.

Wing Personalities

Nines can have either an Eight wing or a One wing. The Referee (9w8) is the more aggressive and forceful of the two subtypes due to having The Challenger as its dominant wing. While all Nines are characterized by their love of peace, tranquility, and cooperation, Referees tend to be more social, active, and open to working in a team environment. The 9w8 is also much more likely to intervene in a conflict and mediate for all of the parties involved. On the other hand, The Dreamer (9w1) is more creative and imaginative, as well as more prone to getting swept away into their fantasies and daydreams. Dreamers have the ability to lean into their One wing and focus on ordering their lives and achieving their goals. The 9w1 is less outgoing and more reserved than their counterparts with an Eight wing. While the 9w8 is perfectly fine with working on a team, the 9w1 more often prefers to work alone. All Nines are independent in some respect, but the wings express this tendency in different ways.

Acceptance

Nines have the ability to see every angle of a conflict without taking sides. They can be impartial in most situations, even ones that affect them personally. On the other hand, Nines tend to merge with other types and lose their own individual identity or preferences due to this same unique quality. It is very easy for them to lose focus, go through the motions of daily life, and retreat rather than take up their own space in the world. Resentment at being ignored or undervalued can also make Nines very passive-aggressive in their interactions with others. It takes a lot to get a Nine to become as aggressive as an Eight, but they are much more prone to giving the subtle clues that they are annoyed or angry. It is also very easy for other types to take advantage the impartiality of Nines. They know that they can get their Nine friend, partner, or colleague to agree to anything since they know they do not like altercations and will likely avoid one.

A Nine's partner needs to be very direct about what it is they want. Asking pointed questions like, "What do *you* want to do?" or "What do *you* think about this?" is key to good communication, and then actually listening to the Nine's answer. Their own individual personality and preferences need to be drawn out in order for the Nine to avoid merging with others and losing their individuality.

II. Enneagram Pairings & Interplay

ONE: The Reformer in Relationships

Ones with Ones

When two of the same type are in a relationship with each other, they have the tendency to amplify each other's shared qualities. Ones are very practical, pragmatic, and place a high value on order. When both partners focus themselves on these things, they can become overly concerned with the more bureaucratic and non-emotional aspects of daily life - work, responsibilities and regular tasks. The more pleasurable things, such as hobbies and vacations, consequently become less important. Ones are also devoted to improvement for themselves, their relationships, their work, and their lives in general. When two Ones combine this devotion, especially if they also share the same wing, they may find themselves never happy with what they have achieved together.

Ones with Twos

Ones and Twos often find themselves paired together, and the combination can make for a very good couple. Ones excel at being practical and organized while Twos value warmth in their relationships. When average or stressed, Ones can view Twos as being too all over the place while Twos might consider Ones to be overly rigid and unyielding. When they learn how to compromise and value each other's contributions to the relationship, the Two types can help each other in very positive ways. Twos struggle with feeling unwanted and at risk of being abandoned. The stability of Ones and their perseverance to honor their commitments can help alleviate a Two's fear of being left on their own. Twos can also help the One to relax and allow their affection for others to show.

Ones with Threes

Ones and Threes in a relationship can face many of the same struggles as a pair of Ones might see in their coupling. Both types are very driven and goal-oriented, and there exists within this dynamic the possibility of letting tasks and achievements become the centerpiece of how they relate to each other. Ones might also get annoyed with Threes because while both are focused on achievement, Threes just want to get the task finished. They are comfortable with taking shortcuts or cutting corners whereas the One is all about doing things the correct way. Directions are important to the One, but they are more like guidelines to the Three. This sense of annoyance can make Ones behave judgmentally toward their Three partner. Ones also do not tend to show much emotion, and Threes often suppress theirs. This can be avoided to an extent if both types have a dominant Two wing that they can actively lean into to help with their emotional health.

Ones with Fours

Ones and Fours can have a very interesting and mutually beneficial relationship. Ones are often very repressed in their emotions, especially when it comes to anger, and they are often characterized by rigidity and excessive order when they are in an average to unhealthy range. Fours meanwhile, are expressive, creative, and emotive. Ones can help Fours stay focused on the present, see things through to the end, and not live so much within their interior emotional landscape. Fours can simultaneously help Ones find their ability to express themselves and see a more fluid and nuanced approach to life rather than simply relying on binary black-and-white thinking.

Ones with Fives

Although Ones and Fives are located in different triads, they have a lot of similarities between them. Both are very objective, pragmatic, and reserved. Both types tend to be very philosophical, although Ones are more likely to believe in an ultimate, objective truth while Fives are more of the opinion that truth is subjective or relative. Fives are often quiet, and they normally have no problem with what some of the other types might call an awkward silence. They may actually not even notice it. Ones often assume what others are thinking and pass judgment on either themselves or others based solely upon that. From Fives, Ones can learn that silence, even an awkward silence, is not an automatically negative thing. Ones can also begin to realize that they are not able to accurately guess what others are thinking.

Ones with Sixes

Ones and Sixes are both hard workers who devote themselves wholeheartedly to whatever task is set before them. They are both very reactive, responsive types. While Sixes are more open to outside influence since they often rely on an authority figure or entity of some kind, Ones are much more inflexible and normally view their own way as the only correct one. As such, Ones are often the more dominant partner within this relationship. Issues can come up when the One and Six move toward their stress points. Ones become more judgmental and critical, and Sixes give into their worries and insecurities. Sixes should learn to take more initiative within the relationship, and Ones need to learn that other ways or methods of doing things can be just as valid as their own.

Ones with Sevens

Along with Twos, Ones pair most commonly with Sevens. These two types also share an integration/disintegration line on the Enneagram. In many ways, Ones and Sevens are opposite types. Sevens are relaxed, spontaneous, and fun-loving while Ones are hard-working, practical, and orderly. When average to healthy, these two types can benefit each other in very constructive ways. Ones can help Sevens become more focused and disciplined while Sevens can help Ones ease up on their excessive need for order and excellence, as well as get them to give into their more playful side.

Ones with Eights

When you look below the surface, Ones and Eights have quite a bit in common. They both perceive the world as either black or white, right or wrong. Both types are very set in their ways and are sure that they are right in most situations. They also tend to react before completely thinking things through. Ones and Eights both see themselves as strongly committed to justice and righting the wrongs of the world. Eights do tend to be more forceful in this regard while Ones are more persevering. A common difficulty with this pairing is that both types like to be in control, so there will have to be some give and take in this regard. Eights admire the One's discipline and commitment to following through while Ones wish they could be as free with their actions and emotions as Eights.

Ones with Nines

Nines and Ones also have a lot in common since they are both located within the Instinctive Center, both repress their anger, and they tend to think things through and mull over ideas for lengthy periods of time. In a relationship, Nines help Ones to become less critical of both themselves and others. At the same time, Ones can help the unfocused Nines to become more focused and direct their actions toward specific, attainable goals. When moving into stress, Ones become judgmental and show more frustration with themselves, while Nines can shut down emotionally and retreat to isolation. This can be a challenging combination when moving into stress.

TWO: The Helper in Relationships

Twos with Ones

Twos are the most relational of all the types on the Enneagram. They always put relationships and how they feel ahead of practicality and order. This can be good for each type since Twos can help their One partners relax and feel more comfortable with showing affection and accepting care and nurture, while Ones can provide a sense of structure that might otherwise be lacking with a lot of Twos. A difficulty with this pairing is that both types, for different reasons, tend to ignore their own wants and needs. Twos constantly put others' needs ahead of their own, and Ones can suppress their own to the point that they are not even aware of them. It can also be easier for these types to find common ground if they share the other's dominant wing; for example, a 2w1 and a 1w2 could more easily relate to each other than a 2w3 and a 1w9.

Twos with Twos

Twos always focus on others rather than on themselves, and a pair of Twos together can reinforce this quality in one another. Twos in a healthy relationship are sensitive to each other's emotional states and needs. They are both open and aware of their own feelings, and they are comfortable expressing themselves fully. Twos are very communicative, so a pair of Helpers can excel at communicating honestly with each other. One difficulty is that Twos are much more accustomed to taking care of others than they are to having others take care of them. It can be a new experience to them when they suddenly have a partner who is as attentive to them as they have always been to everyone else. This is not necessarily negative or unpleasant. One possible pitfall of this dynamic is that average to unhealthy Twos might begin to see each other in a competitive manner as to who can nurture the other more acceptably.

Twos with Threes

Threes are one of the most common types that Twos pair with on the Enneagram. Both of them are concerned with image, how they are perceived by others, and how they present themselves to the world. Twos want to be seen as caring and loving, and Threes want to be viewed as successful. Both Twos and Threes tend to be charismatic individuals with high levels of energy to pursue their goals and interests. They make a good combination because Twos like to celebrate other people, and Threes enjoy being celebrated. Threes can push Twos to put themselves first (which they rarely do) and achieve their own goals. Twos can also help Threes with being loved and validated for who they are rather than simply for what they can accomplish and achieve. Since both types are located in the Feeling Center and are motivated by shame, they will have to learn how to be comfortable with their own vulnerabilities and not retreat from view when they want to hide behind their own particular feelings of inadequacy.

Twos with Fours

Twos and Fours are not a very common pairing when it comes to romantic relationships. It is far more common to find this combination in friendships and professional relationships. But this can still be an interesting and mutually beneficial combination. Fours are the most devoted of all the types on the Enneagram to portraying themselves authentically, which is something that Twos can learn from. Both types are located in the Feeling Center, and they are both comfortable with expressing their emotions. Fours are more comfortable with their darker emotions while Twos prefer the lighter, more carefree ones. Both can learn to express those that the other excels in. Neither type necessarily suppresses how they feel, and they can provide each other with an open space where they can express themselves along with all their cares and worries. One possible difficulty with this pairing is that since both types are so emotionally expressive, there might just be too much emotion to go around. Fours might also find Twos to be too superficial in their positive attitudes, and Twos can view Fours as being too melancholic and melodramatic.

Twos with Fives

This combination can be difficult for a couple of reasons. Fives are the most isolated and private of all the types on the Enneagram. They keep very much to themselves, and they rarely allow others into their own inner world. Fives are intensely private, and many of them could be described as loners. This description rarely, if ever, applies to the Two. Helpers are extremely relational and show a lot of comfort with expressing their emotions. In many ways, Twos and Fives are exact opposites. A Two can sometimes feel rejected by their Five partner because they are just not as responsive as they expect them to be at all times. However, the Five is not necessarily trying to be emotionally distant. If the Two tries to force a response from their partner, they can become intrusive to the Five, which can also make them retreat even further into themselves. Twos must learn to give Fives enough space to open up while Fives should learn to become more open emotionally, for both themselves and their partner.

Twos with Sixes

Twos and Sixes have a lot of similarities, but they have somewhat different emphases. For example, both types are committed to being responsible within their lives, relationships, and communities. Twos focus on building solid friendships and romantic relationships where the other person can feel safe and able to express themselves without fear of judgement. Sixes are more concerned with the tangible things in life that ensure safety and security: work, money, family and community. Both are committed to a strong family, Sixes more for the structure and Twos more for interpersonal relationships. Regardless of the motives, community is important to both of them. Sixes who are average to unhealthy may feel that they are under too much stress or pressure to maintain their own independence. The Two's insistence on more intimacy can also feel threatening to an unhealthy Six, and an unhealthy Two often feels like there is no such thing as too much intimacy.

Twos with Sevens

Both Twos and Sevens are friendly, outgoing, and sociable types. Twos, however, can sometimes feel apprehensive or even intimidated around Sevens because they have so much energy and can move between different people, activities, and ideas with ease. Twos can help Sevens ease up on the constant stream of activities and listen to themselves and their feelings while Sevens can show Twos how to be comfortable with unpredictability and spontaneity. A challenge in this relationship is that the

Two may not feel as if they are being heard or have enough intimacy because Sevens can be so unfocused. Sevens also do not wish to be tied down and have their future options limited. Both Twos and Sevens need to learn how to verbalize what they want and express themselves and their thoughts clearly to one another.

Twos with Eights

Besides Threes, Twos also pair most commonly with Eights. This can be a very good combination, although it might make both parties uncomfortable at first. Twos and Eights share a line of integration/disintegration on the Enneagram, so they often have more in common than meets the eye. Twos admire the authenticity of Eights and their ability to be themselves at all times. Eights also welcome the nurturing presence of Twos which can help them let their guard down and feel more comfortable with accepting affection and feeling vulnerable. Any altercations between these two will likely stem from where they place their most essential values. Twos are the more relational, people-oriented of all the types while Eights are action-oriented and place the highest value on getting things done. This is where they will need to find common ground.

Twos with Nines

Nines and Twos have several points of commonality. They are both oriented toward others, and they enjoy taking care of other people. Neither type likes conflict, and they will strive to avoid it, although for different reasons. One key difference is that Nines are often averse to taking action while Twos usually have much more energy and will jump into almost any situation. This is especially true of the Two if they are helping another person in some way. Both Nines and Twos are laid back, easy to talk to, and friendly. They can encounter conflict when they are unable to talk directly about issues in their relationship. This includes small, seemingly insignificant ones. It can get to the point where a Nine will finally stand up for themselves and voice an opinion that the Two may not necessarily like. Twos do not like criticism or critique. While these two are similar, it is also important that they acknowledge each other's differences.

THREE: The Achiever in Relationships

Threes with Ones

Threes and Ones are both very focused on completing tasks and achieving goals. They are both hard workers and have the ability to put aside their emotions and difficulties to get the job finished. One major difference between the two is that Ones are very focused on completing each step of a task or project as recommended while Threes just want to wrap it up as quickly as possible. Threes are comfortable with cutting corners as long as the finished product is of good quality whereas Ones are not. Ones have a hard time getting used to this, and Achievers need to learn to be patient with their Reformer partners.

Threes with Twos

Threes can often pair themselves with Twos, and they usually make for a good combination. They are both very conscious of the image they project, although their emphases are different. Twos want to be viewed as loving and caring, and Threes desire to be perceived as successful. Especially in a professional relationship, Twos can busy themselves with meeting other people's needs (especially their clients) while Threes focus more on work tasks. This can be a winning combination in both professional and personal relationships. When one or both types are average or have become unhealthy, they can give into their fears and insecurities.

And since both types are in the Feeling Center, many of these insecurities overlap and feed into each other.

Threes with Threes

As with any pairing with two of the same type, they tend to bring out each other's strengths and weaknesses. Threes are one of the most driven of all the types on the Enneagram, and a pair of Threes together can often get carried away with their ambitions. When both partners are healthy, they can make a great team and work together to build each other up and achieve their goals. When one or the other move to their stress points, they can begin to see one another not as partners, but as competition. Threes often struggle with expressing their emotions, so it will be very helpful for each of them to lean into one of their dominant wings. Both Twos and Fours are comfortable with their feelings, so either wing will be helpful in balancing this trait in the Three.

Threes with Fours

Threes and Fours are both located in the Feeling Center, and both are driven in some way by shame. While Fours tend to place too much emphasis on how they are feeling, Threes do not place nearly enough emphasis on this characteristic. Fours can live within their emotions, and Threes might not even be aware that they even have them. Fours can help Threes work through and develop their feelings and how to express them while Threes can aid Fours in letting their emotions go in favor of being diplomatic. This relationship can be especially successful if Threes are able to develop and lean into their Four wing, thus making them more comfortable with their own emotions.

Threes with Fives

Threes and Fives are often paired together in both personal and professional relationships. They can learn a lot from each other, and both can find their relationship mutually beneficial. Both Threes and Fives are committed to excellence in some way, and this often comes out in their professional endeavors. This is where they can find a lot of common ground. Threes are very decisive and action-oriented whereas Fives are far more reserved and need to spend a lot of time alone to process their thoughts and ideas. They can both learn from each other's tendencies and implement the strategies that bring out the best in both of them.

Threes with Sixes

A Three with a Six is not a very frequently seen combination. Both types are hard workers, which they will appreciate in each other. Threes are the optimists in the relationship, and they are also much more energetic than most Sixes. Sixes are often pessimistic, but they are also very loyal. One thing to be cognizant of in this pairing is how the Six can sometimes view the Three. Because Threes are so focused on image, good impressions, and positivity, Sixes might at times see them as superficial and projecting an artificial image for others to admire. This can annoy the Six who often tends to be much more down-to-earth than a typical Three. If one or both partners are not operating at healthy levels, they can reinforce each other's negative qualities.

Threes with Sevens

Threes and Sevens can make for a very successful, energetic couple. Both types are outgoing, enjoy being around people, and are driven to achieve goals in some way. They also tend to be very optimistic. They can each bring their own individual strengths to a relationship as well. Threes are deft when it comes to communication, and Sevens value spontaneity. They can learn these skills from each other. On the other hand, neither type is comfortable with vulnerability nor are they entirely in touch with their emotions. Threes are also extremely work-oriented and can be very ambitious in this area of their lives. Sevens tend to be less concerned with their professional careers than a typical Three. This can be a fun and energetic yet difficult pairing.

Threes with Eights

Threes and Eights can have a similar dynamic to Threes and Sevens. All three of these types are of the aggressive stance, and none of them are particularly in touch with their deeper emotions. Sevens stick to their positive feelings, Eights are comfortable with expressing their anger, and Threes tend to ignore everything. Both Threes and Eights will pursue whatever it is they want in life, and they have nearly endless amounts of self-confidence. Also similar to the previous dynamic, neither of these types show comfort with being vulnerable. They both may put in too many hours at work, becoming distant and eventually annoyed with each other. Unhealthy Eights often try to openly control the people around them, and Threes can become manipulative to get whatever it is they want. While these types are very competitive, it is important for them to refrain from competing with each other if they want the relationship to work.

Threes with Nines

Threes often pair themselves with Nines, and they make for a very complementary relationship. Threes and Nines also share an integration/disintegration line on the Enneagram. Nines are more than willing to take a backseat to the ambitions of the Three, and they will offer support to their partner as they work to reach their goals. The safety and stable atmosphere that Nines offer their partners allows the Three to relax and express themselves emotionally. In daily life, Threes are assertive and work to make things happen while Nines are much more reserved and may simply wait for things to happen in due time. Nines need to learn from Threes to be be more proactive and go after what they want in life, and Threes must learn from Nines to let themselves rest from time to time and take life as it comes. Each type needs each other's energy to grow both as individuals and together.

FOUR: The Individualist in Relationships

Fours with Ones

Fours paired with Ones are one of the more common relationships among Enneagram types. Ones usually present themselves as impartial and unemotional, and they often disassociate themselves from how they feel. This is especially true regarding anger. On the other hand, Fours can be overindulgent and identify too strongly with the entire range of their emotions. Each type can help the other address their weak points by using their own strong points. Fours can teach Ones how to express themselves in healthy, measured ways while Ones can help Fours learn to not identify too strongly with how they are feeling in the moment. Ones can recognize that their emotions are an intrinsic part of who they are, and Fours can realize that they are not solely comprised of them.

Fours with Twos

It is not very common to see the Four and Two pairing in romantic relationships. It is much more common to see them as friends or colleagues. In a lot of ways, they are opposites. Twos go after people, pursuing them with love, affection, and a desire for intimacy. Conversely, Fours tend to run away from people. When Fours feel overwhelmed or unable to process their insecurities or the actions of other people, they pull back and isolate themselves. While both types are part of the Feeling Center and comfortable with expressing themselves, Fours show more ease with their darker emotions. Fours are often characterized as melancholy, sad, or even depressed. Twos are far more comfortable with their lighter, happier emotions. Fours can view Twos as being superficial while Twos can see their Four partners as somber and moody. For a successful relationship, it would be beneficial for the types to sit down and talk through their emotions and how they are feeling.

Fours with Threes

Even though both Fours and Threes are located within the Feeling Center, they approach their emotions in very different ways. Fours go all out in expressing themselves authentically while Threes can disassociate entirely from how they feel. A very emotional type alongside a very unemotional type can make for a difficult relationship, so it is essential that both partners meet somewhere in the middle. This common ground can be easier to find if both partners share each other's dominant wing. Fours can lean into their Three wing to release some of their emotional angst, and Threes can lean into their Four wing so that they feel more at ease when expressing themselves. This pairing can be very mutually beneficial if both partners can find a middle ground.

Fours with Fours

A pairing of two Fours brings together a conisderable amount of emotion to their relationship. This can make for a lot of sensitivity as to how the other Four is feeling and what they might need at any given time. Fours are the type most comfortable with talking about the darker moments in their past and working through the scars of their trauma. This may be a new experience for one or both partners since Fours are the rarest number on the Enneagram, and most other types are not nearly as comfortable with being so raw and unfiltered in their conversations. However, Fours can also be very imbalanced in their emotional expressiveness when they are not healthy. As they move further into stress, Fours have a tendency to play the victim and give into their fear of being abandoned. Both partners need to be honest with each other and work on developing their wings, especially the more logical Five wing located in the Thinking Center. Bringing some Head energy into all of those feelings can have a positive effect for both Fours.

Fours with Fives

Fives pair very well with Fours, and they are one of the most common partners for an Individualist. Fives are logical, unflustered, and capable of remaining non-emotional. Fours can let their feelings run away with them at times, but the Five's steady presence can bring them back down to Earth. In return, a Four can help their Five partner learn to express themselves emotionally and creatively. Both types like to explore their own inner depths as well as topics that they are curious about on an intellectual level. One fairly common difficulty with this pairing is that Fives need a lot of space to tend to themselves, and Fours prefer to have more intimacy and interaction than a Five might be prepared to give. This dynamic will have to be talked through so that each partner feels that they have what they need for a healthy, successful relationship.

Fours with Sixes

Fours and Sixes have several key similarities that can serve them well as a romantic couple or other type of relationship. Both of them feel their emotions very strongly, and they tend to feel misunderstood by those around them in some way. They can also both feel insecure, although for different reasons. Fours' insecurities come out when they doubt themselves and their identity while Sixes feel insecure (or unsafe) with their surroundings. The two can find a common ground here, but it is important that they commit to honest communication and do not take their tendencies to feel misunderstood and apply them to each other. Fours can influence Sixes with their creativity and expressiveness while Sixes can help ground Fours with their work ethic and practicality. The loyal Six can also be a great comfort to their Four partner who is often afraid of being abandoned or left behind.

Fours with Sevens

In many ways, Fours and Sevens are exact opposites on the Enneagram. Depending on the specific relationship, this can have either a very positive dynamic or a very complicated one. Fours tend to be introverted, shy, and self-conscious while Sevens are much more outgoing, extroverted, and eager to try new things. Fours can help Sevens explore their own inner world and the full range of their more serious emotions. Meanwhile, Sevens can also help push their Four partners out of their comfort zone and embrace more spontaneity and the lighter, more carefree emotions of life. Both Fours and Sevens are impulsive in their own unique ways, and this can create problems where one or the other partner is in an unhealthy space. Without honest communication, Fours can become drained by the constant activity of their Seven partner, and Sevens can get annoyed with the Four when they become overly sensitive and hyper-emotional.

Fours with Eights

Fours and Eights are very different types, but they do have some key overlapping qualities. Both types are very emotionally responsive and have a dominant streak of some kind. Fours dominate when it comes to emotions, and Eights are very dominant when they interact socially with others. Honest and open communication is very important to this relationship being able to work out. In particular, Eights need to learn to become emotionally vulnerable. Fours are accepting and welcoming of all emotions, but they do need to limit their dramatic reactions (or overreactions) so that they do not drive their Eight partner away. It is each other's intensity in different areas of their lives that draws these two types together, but it can also drive them away if one or both are in an unhealthy space.

Fours with Nines

Along with Fives, Fours pair most commonly and successfully with Nines. Nines are relaxed and mellow, and their Four partner can bring out their creativity and sense of passion. In return, Nines are receptive to all of the Four's emotional expressiveness, and they will not easily turn away from them. Fours and Nines are perhaps the two most creative types on the Enneagram. They both have the withdrawing stance, which tends to be very introverted, and they often have high, or even romantic, ideals in life. Since both are withdrawing types, Fours and Nines are considered to be "doing repressed." Neither types are naturally proactive, so someone will need to take the initiative at times to get things done. When unhealthy, they also deal with stress in different ways that can possibly annoy their partner or even drive them away. Fours become more emotional and are prone to dramatic outbursts while Nines are more likely to seal themselves away and become uncommunicative.

FIVE: The Investigator in Relationships

Fives with Ones

Fives often find themselves paired with Ones, and they can have a very interesting and beneficial relationship. Both types have similar qualities, such as objectivity and pragmatism. They think before they act. Fives want to have as much information as possible so as to present themselves as knowledgable and well-informed. Ones are devoted to their desire to achieve perfection and not make any missteps. Fives value the independence of Ones. Investigators like to be left to their own devices, and Ones do not feel pushed out by this tendency. Fives are also not a type to be very judgmental, and Ones appreciate this since they can often be very hard on themselves due to their excessive perfectionism.

Fives with Twos

Fives and Twos are perhaps perfect opposites, and they are often found in successful combinations because of this. Fives are the most cerebral and intellectual type on the Enneagram, as well as the most isolated, introverted, and reserved. Twos, located in the Feeling Center, are one of the most open and sociable types, and they often wear their heart on their sleeve. Fives are very strict and measured in their personal boundaries whereas Twos seem to have no boundaries at all. This is a good exercise in development for both types as they hone their interpersonal skills. Because Fives are so independent and need a lot of alone time, Twos can begin to pay more attention to themselves rather than always looking after the needs of others as they normally do. The sociable and extroverted tendencies of Twos can rub off on their Five partner, making them warmer and better able to engage with others. Twos will need to learn to give Fives the space that they need to function, and Fives should learn to become more open with their emotional expressiveness.

Fives with Threes

Fives can often be found in combination with Threes, where they can learn a lot from each other in their relationships. Both types are hard workers, committed to achieving their best both personally and professionally, and they are very good communicators in their own way. Threes tend to be more charming and charismatic while Fives focus on making accurate and precise arguments. Communication and excellence are two areas where Fives and Threes can find common ground. Threes are often very busy individuals, so they normally do not require a lot of intimacy or affection from their partners, which suits Fives quite well. Fives can also help Threes become comfortable with pulling back and withdrawing from their often excessive activities and social engagements. Since both Fives and Threes do not relate very well to their own emotional states, it is important that they talk through how they are feeling and stay on the same page within their relationship.

Fives with Fours

Although Fives and Fours are very different in many ways, they are also capable of finding common ground when they do overlap. Where Fours are emotional, dramatic, and expressive, Fives are logical, stoic, and intellectual. As different as these two types are in temperament, they are both attracted to ideas and topics that have a certain depth to them. Neither are drawn to light or superficial books, films, ideas, or conversations. Fives and Fours are also very withdrawn and introverted, but they can both be drawn out of their shells by the other when they are introduced to new ideas or experiences that also have a unique intensity to them. Fives with a more developed Four wing are also more likely to have a better connection to their Four partner since they will be able to lean more easily into their emotions and feel more comfortable expressing them. When moving into stress, Fives can view Fours as overly dramatic and irrational while Fours might see their Five partners as detached from both their own feelings and the relationship. A consensus will have to be made where Fives can have the space they require and Fours can find the intimacy they need.

Fives with Fives

Fives are probably the type that is most comfortable with their own number, although this relationship can tend to reinforce each other's negative traits. Two very introverted types may never push the other to move outside of their comfort zone. Fives are very sensitive to personal space and others' boundaries, so they are very careful not to cross any lines, especially with other Fives. Being located in the Thinking Center, two very intellectual Fives might also put so much emphasis on thinking that there is very little development of feeling or doing within their relationship. Everything they do or feel might be processed analytically or intellectually rather than through the lens of emotions or physicality. Fives also tend to isolate themselves, but two average or unhealthy Fives may even isolate themselves from one another. To help avoid this, Fives can develop either their more emotional Four wing or their more curious, "others-oriented" Six wing.

Fives with Sixes

Fives and Sixes are both located in the Thinking Center, so they both tend to be drawn to intellectual pursuits and are driven in some way by fear. Both of them are detailed, analytical, and have the ability to be impartial and unbiased when considering a problem or situation. Fives can remain calm and objective in the face of anxiety, and Sixes often need this since they are one of the most anxiety-prone of all the types on the Enneagram. Sixes can often experience irrational fear, and Fives can help talk them through any logical inconsistencies to put them at ease. For Fives, Sixes offer loyalty and faithfulness, which can help keep their more introverted partners from withdrawing too much. When one or both partners become stressed, the relationship can begin to show strain or even break down. Fives often see the Six as being too conservative or limited in their thinking, and Sixes might consider the Five to be too detached and independent.

Fives with Sevens

Fives and Sevens can have a very mutually beneficial relationship. Fives can provide calm, balance, and the ability to observe the playful characteristics of a Seven. Meanwhile, Sevens can help their Five partners lighten up, not take themselves so seriously, and live more spontaneously. Sevens are often so flighty and untethered that they need the grounding of a personality that a Five can offer. Reciprocally, Fives often need to be pushed out of their comfort zone because they tend to withdraw and isolate themselves from many of the more extroverted activities that life has to offer. When both types become unhealthy, they can sometimes drive each other away. Sevens become hyperactive when moving into stress, and this can make the Five become even more reclusive in an attempt to preserve their own energy. Sevens may see unhealthy Fives as detached and unemotional, and Fives in return might see their Seven partners as superficial. They will need to engage in honest communication in order to find common ground and a way forward.

Fives with Eights

Fives and Eights have a lot of opposite qualities that they can bring to their relationship. Fives are very intellectual and live inside their minds whereas Eights have a very strong physicality and express themselves through movement and action. An Eight can help their Five partner reconnect with their body and move beyond their very well developed mental functions. Similarly, Fives can help Eights align more with their mental processes and rely less on their physical expressiveness. Eights are also very forceful whereas Fives, tend to isolate themselves and retreat from many social functions. Eights can help their Five partners identify more strongly with themselves and define who they are and what they want from life. Fives, being the more restrained partner in the relationship, can help Eights discover how to limit themselves when necessary, think before acting, and develop their processes of thinking and observing. When these two types move into the unhealthy regions of their personalities, both Fives and Eights can feel a strong sense of rejection and become cynical.

Fives with Nines

Fives and Nines make for a good combination because both types are introverted, relaxed, and have learned to give other people the space that they themselves value. Nines are very laid back individuals, so they are not likely to pressure Fives to move too far outside of their comfort zone. They will not force their Five partner to do something that they are not yet comfortable with. However, most Nines are also independent enough that they will not always agree to everything a Five does or says. While also introverted and reserved, Nines are the warmer and more affectionate of the two types. This warmth and nurturing presence can help Fives open themselves up to more emotional expressiveness. One challenge with this combination is that because both types are so independent and accustomed to giving a large amount of space to others, they will rarely push the other to try new things or take the initiative in many important situations. As one or both types move into stress, they can even begin isolating from each other.

SIX: The Loyalist in Relationships

Sixes with Ones

Sixes and Ones are both responsible and committed hard workers. Both types have strong personal ethics and ideals that they try to uphold in their daily lives. For Ones, those ethics are more intrinsic to how they view the world, while Sixes tend to seek validation from an authority outside of themselves. This makes Ones more confident in themselves since their values are held more closely to their very identity. Ones also tend to be the lead in the relationship for this very reason. Ones are also known as The Perfectionist, and they have very high standards in almost every area of their lives. Sixes often do not feel like they can measure up to Ones' code of conduct, and this can give them a certain sense of anxiety. Sixes are already the most anxious of all the Enneagram numbers, so this relationship dynamic may only add to it. An unhealthy One who becomes more critical of themselves and those around them can add to the anxiety that a Six might feel. In order to move toward health and make the relationship work, Sixes need to become more independent and take more initiative.

Sixes with Twos

Sixes and Twos share many traits that can set the stage for a successful relationship. Both types value family. The Six values the structure it provides in life and the Two values the familial relationships it fosters. In life as well as relationships, Sixes are always focused on safety and security whereas Twos are preoccupied with other people and relationships. Sometimes these goals might conflict, so the two partners will need to find common ground that is acceptable to both of them. Because Sixes are so guarded and careful with everything in their lives, they often doubt the motivations of other people or what they might be thinking. With the Two, their motivations are almost always pure when it comes to their relationships. They may want to endear themselves to the Six so that they will be loved and wanted, but that is the extent of their ulterior motives. Sixes also value their independence while Twos desire more intimacy, so this dynamic will have to be worked out so that each partner is happy.

Sixes with Threes

Sixes do not pair very often with Threes, especially when it comes to romantic relationships. Both of them work hard and focus on achievement and value the lack of laziness in the other. Threes are one of the most optimistic types on the Enneagram, and they love to be successful. It is what they work for more than anything else. On the other hand, Sixes are perhaps the most pessimistic of all the types, and they do not trust success, including their own. Sixes can help Threes not put too much stock in how successful they have managed to be, and Threes can help Sixes find more optimism in life and perhaps value their own successes more. When unhealthy, Sixes might regard the Three as shallow and superficial, and Threes can view Sixes as nervous and anxiety-ridden. Both types can repress their emotions for different reasons, so they will need to keep talking through how they are feeling.

Sixes with Fours

Sixes and Fours can find several points of common ground in their relationships. Both types tend to feel misunderstood in some way by those around them, and they often strongly feel their own insecurities. Sixes feel insecure or unsafe when it comes to their surroundings or the people in their lives. They find it difficult to trust. On the other hand, Fours feel insecure with themselves and their identity. As the most most anxious type on the Enneagram, Sixes often give themselves over to playing through hypothetical worst-case scenarios in their minds, whereas Fours are far more comfortable with their pessimism. They can wallow in their melancholy emotions and longing without necessarily being depressed. In their relationship, Sixes can help ground Fours with more practical thinking and the responsibility to see their tasks through to the end while Fours can bring more creative freedom and expressiveness to their Six partners.

Sixes with Fives

Sixes and Fives are both intellectual types located in the Thinking Center. They each have the capacity to analyze, pay attention to details, and show impartiality in making a decision or considering an issue that concerns them. Sixes like to have all the answers, and they actively search for reassurance outside of themselves. Fives are more comfortable with not having the answers to everything, but they love being in pursuit of them. Sixes are one of the most fearful and anxious types on the Enneagram, and Fives can help them with their calming, objective presence. In return, Sixes are the most loyal of all the types. With a loyal partner who won't let them slip into an unhealthy isolation, Fives can become more comfortable with moving outside of their comfort zone from time to time. Under stress, Sixes might view their Five partner as being too impartial and detached from real life while Fives might view Sixes as being too limited in their points of view.

Sixes with Sixes

As with any of the double relationships on the Enneagram, two Sixes usually reinforce their shared qualities with each other. Since type Six is the most fearful and anxious of all the types, dual Sixes are often able to relate to each other over their shared fears and anxieties. Each Six seems to finally realize that they are understood by someone who has the same insecurities that they have always had. It is important that at least one of the partners in this relationship remains healthy, since their fears can easily feed into one another. Sixes are also prone to always expect the worst, draw up doomsday scenarios in their minds, and develop a scarcity mindset where nothing will ever be enough to make them feel safe and secure. Two Sixes in an unhealthy relationship can become consumed by suspicions about each other and worry about the future.

Sixes with Sevens

Sixes and Sevens are both located in the Thinking Center, and they have a lot of traits that reinforce each other and help each other grow. Sevens are one of the most optimistic and cheerful types on the Enneagram, and they can help pull the far more pessimistic Sixes out of any ruts they might get themselves into. Sixes are much more practical than their Seven partners, so they can take the necessary steps to put Sevens' somewhat far-fetched plans and ideas into action. Sixes can also be quite fearful and show a lot of perhaps unwarranted anxiety. Sevens can help their Six partners put their fears into perspective and begin mastering them. When imagining the future, both types are imaginative: Sevens for the better and Sixes for the worse. When unhealthy, Sevens often view Sixes as too anxious and consumed by their fears while Sixes see Sevens as too flighty and preoccupied by their every whim.

Sixes with Eights

Sixes and Eights are both very loyal to their friends, family, and partners. Sixes can sometimes be loyal to a fault, especially when they are unhealthy. Sixes and Eights both struggle with issues of trust. They always have a sense of unease about how safe and secure they are, and Eights constantly struggle with issues of vulnerability and the fear of being controlled. If they can find common ground here and are able to put their trust in one another, they can build a strong and lasting relationship. While both types are capable of feeling strong emotions, they also tend to hide them. Neither type wants to appear vulnerable. Eights want to be seen as strong with a tough exterior while Sixes are all about being on the defensive as a tactic to maintain security. A difficulty with Eights and Sixes who are average to healthy is that Eights move too quickly for most Sixes and Sixes are too measured in their actions for most Eights. They will need to communicate and find a common ground where they can come together.

Sixes with Nines

Sixes pair very well with Nines, and this is one of the most common combinations for the Six. They share a line of integration/disintegration on the Enneagram, and in many ways, the two types can see themselves in each other. Nines value peace and tranquility, and this can ease a lot of the pressure that Sixes place upon themselves. Sixes are more sociable and outgoing, and this can push the Nine to move outside of their comfort zone with their loyal Six partner at their side. When one or both partners are average to unhealthy, communication can dry up and they may struggle to maintain open dialogue and interact with each other in positive ways. Both Sixes and Nines have a tendency to wait around for the other one to make a decision rather than taking the initiative on their own. It is important in this relationship that each partner maintains a sense of independence and that dialogue remains open between the two.

SEVEN: The Enthusiast in Relationships

Sevens with Ones

Sevens and Ones can make for a very complementary pair. They share a line on the Enneagram, and they can each learn a lot from the other. Sevens are exciting and vivacious individuals, and they can help the perfectionistic Ones lighten up a bit and indulge in some spontaneity from time to time. On the other hand, Sevens can learn how to engage in better self-control and the ability to finish tasks from their One partner. When these types move toward their stress points, the sometimes overly disciplined Ones can start to view their Seven partner as too shallow and uncommitted. In return, stressed Sevens might consider Ones to be too rigid and judgmental. Talking through the issues and keeping lines of communication open is a key to this relationship remaining healthy.

Sevens with Twos

Sevens and Twos have quite a few similarities. Both types are usually quite extroverted individuals, enjoy the company of others, and tend to be idealists of some kind. Sevens are the most adventurous and spontaneous of all the Enneagram types, and Twos can help them step back and listen to themselves and what they want to do rather than just jumping from one activity to the next. In turn, Sevens can help their Two partners discover how to live in the moment and embrace spontaneity. Difficulties with this pairing arise when the Seven feels tied down and unable to move as freely as they wish they could. Twos also tend to want more intimacy and down time than the Seven might be able to offer. Twos struggle with the fear of being unwanted or unloved, so they need to focus on trusting their partner more. Sevens are also constantly striving after more and new experiences. They should work on sharing that love of new things with their Two partner.

Sevens with Threes

On the surface, Sevens and Threes seem a lot alike. They are both examples of the aggressive stance, both tend to be very extroverted, and they are highly driven to achieve whatever their goals might be. However, Sevens and Threes do have key differences that need to be taken into account within their relationship. Threes are more driven by success for the sake of status, and they are very good communicators. Sevens are motivated more by spontaneity and living in the moment for their own sense of adventure. Neither type likes to limit themselves, but what they don't like to limit is a bit different. Sevens like to keep their options open, whereas Threes do not like to be told that they have to stop working. When unhealthy, Sevens may view their Three partners as workaholics who are inattentive within their personal relationships while Threes may think their Seven partners have no work ethic.

Sevens with Fours

Fours have a tendency to be a little pessimistic at times and see the glass as half empty rather than half full as the Seven normally does. Sevens are the most optimistic type on the Enneagram. Fours tend to doubt themselves and their capacities while Sevens jump in head first with a zeal for life and all that it might offer them. Both Fours and Sevens are passionate and emotional in their own unique ways. Fours are more interior, searching for creativity and authenticity while pushing the boundaries for both. Sevens are extroverted individuals who want to experience as much as possible firsthand. These two types can find common ground they share while also understanding the differences between them. When average to unhealthy, Fours can find the constant activity of their Seven partner to be exhausting, and Sevens can get find the hypersensitivity of Fours to be an annoyance.

Sevens with Fives

Sevens and Fives share a line on the Enneagram, and they can learn a lot from each other to strengthen both themselves individually as well as their relationship. Sevens are passionate, extroverted individuals who can help push the isolated and withdrawn Five out of both their shell and their comfort zone. Fives can provide the grounding and calming balance to the Seven that they are often lacking. In many ways, Fives and Sevens are opposites. They can use their own unique skills to help their partner enhance their weaker points and grow as a person. When moving toward their stress points, Sevens become even more active and scattered which can annoy the Five. Fives may also isolate themselves, making sure that they have enough energy to complete their tasks. This makes them seem detached and reclusive to their Seven partner. Although this partnership does tend to mesh well, they will still need to communicate in order to keep each other on the same page.

Sevens with Sixes

Sevens are perennial optimists, but Sixes can always be counted on to imagine things will be worse than expected. Sixes are the more practical of the two personalities, and they can be a grounding influence on the Seven who tends to be more scattered in their actions and endeavors. While Sevens can be fearful of things like sadness or melancholy, they are much more inclined to venture into unknown territory when trying new things or meeting new people. This can be a very good influence on their Six partner who tends to be fearful and apprehensive of such things. The cheerful exterior of Sevens can help put the anxieties of most Sixes to rest. When average to unhealthy, Sevens might consider the Six to be too fearful and anxious, whereas Sixes look at their Seven partners and see a shallow individual with no sense of responsibility. As they move toward health, these two types can balance each other out and learn from their partner's strengths.

Sevens with Sevens

Sevens are high-energy individuals who like to keep their options open. They don't like to make commitments, which they often view as limiting, nor do they like it when their daily life becomes too regular or predictable. In short, Sevens do not like routines, nor do they like to be limited by others or limit themselves. Sevens prefer to have the wide world of possibilities open to them. In a relationship together, these free spirits will refuse to impose rules or restrictions on each other. Because Sevens flee from difficulties and the darker range of their emotions, maintaining a relationship when it hits its inevitable bumps can be a real task for two Sevens. However, if they want to see their relationship through, they need to stick with the more unpleasant aspects of it and work through their difficulties.

Sevens with Eights

Sevens and Eights are both highly independent, energized, and extroverted individuals. They are both aggressive stance types, which move against people, although the Seven is in the Thinking Center motivated by fear and the Eight is in the Instinctive Center governed by anger. Because of these differences in motivation, Sevens tend to think before they act while Eights are more impulsive and often act without thinking things through first. A Seven and Eight together in a relationship will be highly active and able to get a lot accomplished, both personally and professionally. Sevens are lighter and more carefree than most Eights, so they can take the edge off of the Eight's abrasiveness.

Eights are more direct than their Seven partners, and they are more able and willing to deal with the hard situations that Sevens often flee from. When moving toward their stress points, Eights can turn to bullying to get what they want while Sevens can become flippant and dismissive. Both types act in these ways in order to avoid being controlled by the other. Sevens can lean into their Six wing in order to move away from their anger and impulsiveness while Eights should develop their Nine wing, allowing them to rely more on their own inner peace and tranquillity.

Sevens with Nines

Sevens are commonly found in relationships with Nines, and they tend to have a very healthy dynamic. Sevens are happy and cheerful types that can help the Nine break out of their shell and become more sociable and comfortable in groups. Nines, being the calm and measured type, can help Sevens relax and live in the present moment rather than constantly flitting here and there in search of the next thing that they cannot possibly miss. Sevens can aid Nines in becoming more self-assertive, and Nines can help Sevens become more self-aware. One of the more common difficulties with this relationship is that neither type is very skilled at dealing with arguments or altercations. Sevens will flat out run away and do almost anything else than something that they do not enjoy. Nines will simply ignore a problem until it grows too unmanageable to keep putting off. Both Sevens and Nines will need to learn how to face their fears, preferably together.

EIGHT: The Challenger in Relationships

Eights with Ones

Eights and Ones have much in common. They are both members of the Instinctive Center, so they are both motivated by anger. Eights show their anger freely with little fear of the consequences, whereas Ones suppress their anger. Both types are set in their ways, fully committed to what they believe in, and they are both energetic and tireless in the pursuit of what is important to them. Eights and Ones see what is wrong in the world, and they both commit themselves to changing it for the better. As far as romantic relationships go, this combination is not very common. Both like to be in control, and neither likes to be controlled by anyone else. It is much more likely that Ones and Eights will find themselves as good friends or colleagues.

Eights with Twos

Eights can often be found in relationship with Twos. They share a line on the Enneagram with Eights integrating toward Two and Twos disintegrating toward Eight. Both types have great people skills, and they can be immensely kind and generous, especially when they are in the healthier regions of their personality. Eights especially are affected positively by being in a relationship with Twos. They need the welcoming care and gentle presence of the Two in order to feel safe with their own vulnerability.

Twos in return can learn from the Eight's forceful personality and commitment to being authentic and true to themselves. When moving toward their stress points, Eights become more abrasive and argumentative while Twos try to possess the people around them. Eights do not like being controlled, and Twos shudder at the thought of verbal altercations. The ability to overcome their differences is there, but they will have to put in the effort and actively work towards finding common ground.

Eights with Threes

Eights get along very well with Threes. They are both dynamic, energetic, and outgoing types. While they are located in different centers on the Enneagram, Eights and Threes both share the aggressive stance and are oriented toward the future. Both types like to try new things, live on the edge, and express themselves confidently. While Eights are comfortable with expressing their emotions, most notably when it comes to anger, Threes tend to suppress how they are feeling to the point that they may be unaware of their emotional state. When these two move toward their respective stress points, Eights may try to control their Three partner while Threes will attempt to manipulate those around them to get what they want. These two Enneagram types are more often friends or colleagues as opposed to romantic partners. But whatever their relationship is, they should refrain from competing with each other. Both types tend to be quite competitive, but if they want to work together constructively, they should focus that streak on others rather than each other.

Eights with Fours

Fours are often overly emotional for Eights to deal with at first, but below the surface, these two types actually have a lot in common and can learn from each other. Both have an intense energy to them, and they are drawn to passion and feeling. They also value honesty and are intuitive to the other's needs. Eights struggle with allowing themselves to be vulnerable, and Fours are accepting of all emotions, no matter how dark or destructive they might be. Fours can provide a safe place for Eights to be themselves. Eights are also far more practical and grounded than most Fours, so they can provide the structure that a lot of Individualists need in order to move forward in life. When moving toward their stress points, both types can become overly dramatic and destructive. It is important that each of them learns how to step back and calm down before saying or doing something they might later regret.

Eight with Fives

Eights and Fives have a lot of opposite qualities that they can bring to their relationship in order to benefit the other and help them grow. Fives are calming, thoughtful, and know how to take their time to get things done. They can help their Eight partner slow down and take their time rather than rushing into everything without thinking things through. Being in the Instinctive Center, Eights are physically strong and live in their bodies rather than in their minds. They can help their Five partner get out of their head so much and center themselves more within their physicality. When these two begin disintegrating, Fives become more reclusive and isolate themselves both physically and emotionally from their partner. Eights can become emotionally and even physically destructive. Both Eights and Fives also have the tendency to become cynical when they feel that they have been rejected.

Eights with Sixes

Eights and Sixes are both very loyal types. They remain true to their friends, family, partners, and colleagues. Sixes are motivated by fear, and they often feel uneasy with their surroundings. They have a hard time trusting the people, places, and atmospheres around them. On the other hand, Eights are very confident. Even when they are unhealthy and don't feel secure in themselves, they still manage to give off an air of confidence. Eights in particular struggle with allowing themselves to be vulnerable, and Sixes are constantly on the defensive because of their obsession with security. While Eights often jump into something new without thinking things through all the way, or even at all, Sixes take their time and complete their tasks methodically. The slower pace of Sixes is a good lesson for Eights. They often need to think before taking action. Meanwhile, the confidence of Eights can greatly benefit Sixes who often doubt themselves and feel insecure in their surroundings. Eights are an aggressive stance which is future-oriented while Sixes live much more in the present moment. They can learn a lot from each other about how to interact in both the present and the future.

Eights with Sevens

Eights and Sevens are both aggressive stance types, so they are oriented around the future. They are both independent, full of energy, and highly active. This is even more accentuated if they share each other's wings.

A 7w6 and an 8w9 are both more relaxed and tranquil than a 7w8 and an 8w7 would be. For those two, there is always a level of being constantly on the move. Since Sevens are a thinking type, they do tend to deliberate before taking action. Eights, on the other hand, rarely think before doing. They lead from their gut, and they are the most forceful of the three types located in the Instinctive Center. Eights and Sevens tend to make better friends or colleagues than romantic partners, but it can still work. Each should focus on developing their opposite wings. This can help them draw different, softer energies into their highly active relationship.

Eights with Eights

Two Eights are a very active, passionate, and energetic pairing. They are the most extroverted and dynamic of all the types on the Enneagram, so having two of them together reinforces these personal qualities. Since both types are so forceful, they can drive each other to pursue their goals and activities. Eights are often on the lookout for someone who can match them in their energy and passion, and another Eight can often accomplish this task. Eights with different wings can also appear as very different personalities. Nine wings will soften the Eight quite a bit, and they will value more peace, tranquility, and down time than an Eight with a Seven wing would. An 8w7 is much more active and on the go than their Nine-wing counterpart. It can be helpful to this extremely active relationship if one partner is more willing to look inside themselves and get in touch with their inner emotions. An 8w9 is more capable of accomplishing this task.

Eights with Nines

Eights pair very well with Nines, with this being one of the more common combinations for the Eight. They both bring qualities to the relationship that the other needs. While both types are located in the Instinctive Center, there are vast differences between these two. Eights are the most active of all the types, prone to anger and strong displays of emotion, and they are tireless in working toward their goals. Nines are the least active of the types. They fall asleep to their anger, barely noticing its presence, and often procrastinate in pursuit of their goals.

Nines tend to merge with every other type on the Enneagram, but even more so with Eights because of the sheer force of their personalities. This merging can also help them become more outgoing and develop their Eight wing. In return, Nines give Eights a safe place to be themselves, express how they are feeling, and teach them how to rest from time to time. In stress, Eights may become even more forceful and aggressive, which can make Nines turn away from the relationship and shut themselves off from any further interaction. It is important for these two to communicate honestly about what they are thinking and feeling.

NINE: The Peacemaker in Relationships

Nines with Ones

Nines can very commonly be found paired with Ones. Both can learn a lot and benefit from each other. Nines tend to be very lax in their routines and struggle with being proactive. These are two areas where Ones excel, and they can help their Nine partners hone these skills. In return, Nines can aid Ones in becoming gentler and less critical. Ones are very critical of others but more especially of themselves. They can learn kindness and self-acceptance from their Peacemaker partner. Nines prefer peace and harmony over being right or correct, and this quality can also help ease the One's anxieties about their perfectionism. At the same time, Ones can help Nines leave behind their lethargy and move into a more active role in their own lives. When these two move toward their stress points, Ones become overly critical and judgmental while Nines can shut themselves off emotionally. Nines and Ones need to be honest with their feelings and learn to find common ground during disagreements.

Nines with Twos

Along with Ones, Twos are the most commonly paired Enneagram type for Nines. And they have a lot of similarities that can make for a successful relationship. Both types are "others-oriented". They enjoy the company of other people and are concerned about their welfare. Twos are more extroverted with their affection, and Nines are much more introverted when it comes to their concern for someone else. Nines and Twos are both easygoing, friendly, and sensitive individuals. Neither likes conflict, although for different reasons. Twos want everyone to be happy and well taken care of while Nines reject conflicts and arguments of any kind. They value peace and tranquility while Twos value healthy relationships. At their best, Nines can help Twos see where they have crossed boundaries with people. Twos often desire so much intimacy that they may not take notice of any boundaries. In return, Twos can use their more extroverted and sociable personalities to push Nines out of their isolated comfort zones.

Nines with Threes

Nines and Threes, along with Sixes, share lines of integration and disintegration on the Enneagram. They are part of their own triangular microcosm on the diagram, and they share many of each other's traits at their varying levels of health. Nines and Threes can often be found together. The extroverted and sociable personalities of Threes can help push Nines out of their isolation. Nines often seal themselves away from the world in order to maintain their own levels of comfort. From Threes, they can learn to develop their own confidence to step out into the open. In return, Nines can help Threes learn how to relax, take time for themselves, and listen to how they are feeling. When one or both partners are unhealthy, they may tend to ignore conflicts, sadness, or anger. Both types tend to be so positive that they do not like risking negativity, but they need to talk things through in order to maintain a healthy relationship.

Nines with Fours

The combination of Nines and Fours can make for a good partnership or relationship. Although Nines are in the Instinctive Center and Fours are in the Feeling Center, both types have the withdrawing stance. Because of this, they are both "doing repressed." Neither one is known for being very proactive, and Nines in particular struggle with taking the initiative to complete a task or achieve a goal. Being so creative, Fours are capable of bringing out the creativity of Nines who have let that part of themselves lie dormant. They can help them feel more emotionally expressive. In return, Nines are one of the most understanding and accepting of all the types on the Enneagram, and Fours often feel misunderstood by everyone around them. When these types move toward their respective stress points, they deal with their insecurities in contrasting ways. Fours can become hypersensitive and overly dramatic while Nines ignore their anger and refuse to communicate or express their true emotional state.

Nines with Fives

Nines and Fives are also two withdrawing stance types, although Fives tend to be the more isolated and reclusive of the two. Both are adept at giving other people space, especially those with a similar temperament to themselves. Neither type wants to be pushed too far outside of their comfort zone, so they are both cognizant of what their partner is capable of handling when it comes to being sociable or more outgoing. Nines are the warmer and more affection of the two types, and they can help Fives become more open and comfortable with their emotions and expressiveness. They provide a safe place for Fives to exist. Fives are also more structured, and they can help their Nine partners become more organized as well. Nines often do not verbalize themselves very effectively; they live much more comfortably within the realm of feeling. But it is important that Nines learn how to put what they want and need into words for their Five partners to understand clearly.

Nines with Sixes

Nines and Sixes go very well together, and they can contribute to a very healthy, constructive relationship. They share a line of integration and disintegration on the Enneagram, along with the Three, so there are many traits between them that they need to develop as they move toward health. Nines are very reserved and tend to isolate themselves in an attempt to preserve their energy. Sixes are more sociable than their Nine partners, and they can help them step out of their shells and become more outgoing. Nines are also very trusting and tend to believe everyone and everything at face value. Sixes can help Nines understand that not everyone or everything can be trusted by first appearances alone. Being the most relaxed and peaceful of all the types, Nines can help Sixes find tranquility and let their anxieties go. Both types are not adept at saying what they are really thinking, so it is key for these two to talk through how they are feeling and not hold anything back.

Nines with Sevens

Nines and Sevens go together very well, and they have a very interesting, mutually beneficial relationship. Even though their temperaments are quite different, both types are very open-minded, nonjudgmental, and value diversity and differences of opinion. Sevens are extroverted, outgoing, friendly, and cheerful. They can help draw Nines out of their far more introverted shell and become more comfortable with social interactions. Nines value peace, quiet, harmony, and tranquility. They have the ability to help Sevens relax and ease into taking time for themselves rather than always being on the go. Most importantly, Nines are very observant and keep track of what the consequences are for taking certain actions. Sevens generally do not excel at this type of thing, so Nines can be a great help to them. One area of difficulty with the dynamic of this relationship is that each type avoids confrontation or arguments for their own reasons. Nines want things to remain peaceful, and Sevens do not like to experience anything that is not positive. They will need to work together to learn how to overcome their own individual shortcomings.

Nines with Eights

Nines and Eights make very good partners in a relationship. They are one of the more common pairings for Eights. Both types are located in the Instinctive Center, but they have very different temperaments. Eights are bold, decisive, and energetic. They are perhaps the most driven number on the Enneagram. On the other hand, Nines are the most relaxed, reserved, and inactive of all the types. Even Nines with a dominant Eight wing are more reserved than most other numbers. Eights can help Nines become more proactive in their lives, working to achieve goals and develop routines for themselves. In return, Nines provide their Eight partners with a safe place to be vulnerable. Nines are very accepting individuals, and they can teach Eights how to relax and take time for themselves. In a relationship, it is important for Nines to set their own parameters. They tend to go along with what everyone else wants, and especially for an Eight, the most dominant of all the types, there is the chance that they will let their partner outline their relationship.

Nines with Nines

Nines are the most common number on the Enneagram to pair with their own type. Nines are often drawn to each other because of their laid back personality, gentleness, and ability to give their partner space, which is exactly what another Nine wants as well. Nines like to take things as they come, but they prefer their lives to be predictable. They don't really care to be thrown off center. The goal of many Nine couples is to create a safe space for themselves, and then continue to live in it as peacefully as possible. A drawback to this relationship is that neither one wants to take the initiative when something more difficult, strenuous, or stressful must be done. There is so much conflict-avoidance with two Nines that issues can be pushed aside and ignored until they become unmanageable. To remedy this, it is important for Nines to lean into either their Eight wing or their One wing in order to use those skills in becoming more proactive individuals.

CONCLUSION

The Enneagram is a complex system of human personality. In its modern incarnation, it exists to help individuals understand themselves and eventually their relationship to others. Once you have discovered your dominant type and stronger wing, you can begin exploring how you behave in both health and stress. You can also begin to observe how you interact with others in your different levels of health, and how their own Enneagram type could be an influence in your relationships. This can be most useful in close relationships, and especially romantic ones. If you are not currently in a relationship, the same Enneagram teachings can also help you understand which types and what kind of person might suit you best in the future.

Each Enneagram type has their own individual journey through life, complete with their own unique difficulties, weaknesses, triggers, and insecurities, that they must learn to overcome and eventually turn into their own unique strengths. If you are aware of your type, as well as that of your partner, then you will be more conscious and cognizant of what should be both developed and avoided in order to build the strongest and most lasting relationship possible. If you are also aware of the direction in which you and your partner integrate in health or disintegrate in stress, then you will both be able to catch yourselves descending into the lower regions of your personalities before your relationship might be irrevocably harmed.

After reading this book, you should have a clearer idea as to how each Enneagram number interacts in their various relationships with each of the other types. You should also have discovered more about your own number, as well as how you may interact with other people in your life based on their types. You can also apply what you have learned about yourself in future relationships of any kind - personal, professional, and romantic - in order to have the strongest and most lasting interactions possible. The aim of this book has been to provide the reader with a framework with which they can better understand themselves by using the teachings of the Enneagram, as well as to help them understand themselves in relationship with others. Taking what you learn from the Enneagram to heart in this way can improve communication, understanding, empathy, and compassion within relationships of all kinds, but most notably in romantic relationships.

Every relationship has its own difficulties and challenges. The Enneagram can be used to ease some of them and encourage both individual and interpersonal growth. Learning about yourself through the lens of the Enneagram, about your own strengths and weaknesses, and about how you interact with other people based on their unique types, is a lifelong process. There are layers to the Enneagram that can take years, if not an entire lifetime, to completely peel back and understand to their depths. Good luck on your discovery!

BIBLIOGRAPHY

Riso, Don Richard and Russ Hudson. *The Wisdom of the Enneagram: The Complete Guide to Psychological and Spiritual Growth for the Nine Personality Types.* New York, New York: Bantam Books, 1999.

Barron Hall, S. (March 2, 2020). *Communication Styles by Enneagram Type.* Nine Types. https://ninetypes.co/blog/communication-styles-by-enneagram-type

The Enneagram Institute. (2021). *1 - The REFORMER Enneagram Type One.* https://www.enneagraminstitute.com/type-1

- The Enneagram Institute. (2021). *2 - THE HELPER Enneagram Type Two.* https://www.enneagraminstitute.com/type-2

- The Enneagram Institute. (2021). *3 - THE ACHIEVER Enneagram Type Three.* https://www.enneagraminstitute.com/type-3

- The Enneagram Institute. (2021). *4 - THE INDIVIDUALIST Enneagram Type Four.* https://www.enneagraminstitute.com/type-4

- The Enneagram Institute. (2021). *5 - THE INVESTIGATOR Enneagram Type Five.* https://www.enneagraminstitute.com/type-5

- The Enneagram Institute. (2021). *6 - THE LOYALIST Enneagram Type Six.* https://www.enneagraminstitute.com/type-6

- The Enneagram Institute. (2021). *7 - THE ENTHUSIAST Enneagram Type Seven.* https://www.enneagraminstitute.com/type-7

- The Enneagram Institute. (2021). *8 - THE CHALLENGER Enneagram Type Eight.* https://www.enneagraminstitute.com/type-8

- The Enneagram Institute. (2021). *9 - THE PEACEMAKER Enneagram Type Nine.* https://www.enneagraminstitute.com/type-9

- The Enneagram Institute. (2021). *36 Type Misidentifications.* https://www.enneagraminstitute.com/36-type-misidentifications

- Enneagram Paths. (July 23, 2018). *Enneagram 2w1 vs. 2w3.* https://enneagrampaths.com/2018/07/23/enneagram-2w1-vs-2w3/

Nguyen, J. (July 23, 2020). *The Best Ways to Support Your Romantic Partner, Based on Their Enneagram.* Mind Body Green. https://www.mindbodygreen.com/articles/what-to-know-about-dating-each-enneagram-type

Psychologia. (n.d.) *Enneagram 1w2: The One with a Two-Wing.* https://psychologia.co/1w2/

- Psychologia. (n.d.) *Enneagram 1w9: The One with a Nine-Wing.* https://psychologia.co/1w9/

- Psychologia. (n.d.) *Enneagram 1w2: The Two with a One-Wing.* https://psychologia.co/2w1/

- Psychologia. (n.d.) *Enneagram 2w3: The Two with a Three-Wing.* https://psychologia.co/2w3/

- Psychologia. (n.d.) *Enneagram 3w2: The Three with a Two-Wing.* https://psychologia.co/3w2/

- Psychologia. (n.d.) *Enneagram 3w4: The Three with a Four-Wing.* https://psychologia.co/3w4/

- Psychologia. (n.d.) *Enneagram 4w3: The Four with a Three-Wing.* https://psychologia.co/4w3/

- Psychologia. (n.d.) *Enneagram 4w5: The Four with a Five-Wing.* https://psychologia.co/4w5/

- Psychologia. (n.d.) *Enneagram 5w4: The Five with a Four-Wing.* https://psychologia.co/5w4/

- Psychologia. (n.d.) *Enneagram 5w6: The Five with a Six-Wing.* https://psychologia.co/5w6/

- Psychologia. (n.d.) *Enneagram 6w5: The Six with a Five-Wing.* https://psychologia.co/6w5/

- Psychologia. (n.d.) *Enneagram 6w7: The Six with a Seven-Wing.* https://psychologia.co/6w7/

- Psychologia. (n.d.) *Enneagram 7w6: The Seven with a Six-Wing.* https://psychologia.co/7w6/

- Psychologia. (n.d.) *Enneagram 7w8: The Seven with an Eight-Wing.* https://psychologia.co/7w8/

- Psychologia. (n.d.) *Enneagram 8w7: The Eight with a Seven-Wing.* https://psychologia.co/8w7/

- Psychologia. (n.d.) *Enneagram 8w9: The Eight with a Nine-Wing.* https://psychologia.co/8w9/

- Psychologia. (n.d.) *Enneagram 9w1: The Nine with a One-Wing.* https://psychologia.co/9w1/

- Psychologia. (n.d.) *Enneagram 9w8: The Nine with an Eight-Wing.* https://psychologia.co/9w8/

Rowles, Kristi. (n.d.) *Each Enneagram Type at Their Most Healthy & Unhealthy.* Full & Free Enneagram Coaching. https://kristirowles.com/best-worst/

Shatto, R. (September 16, 2020). *Here's What Your Enneagram Type Says About Your Communication Skills.* Elite Daily. https://www.elitedaily.com/p/heres-what-your-enneagram-type-says-about-your-communication-skills-34117530

Storm, S. (August 6, 2020). *Integration, Disintegration, and Your Enneagram Type.* Psychology Junkie. https://www.psychologyjunkie.com/2020/08/06/enneagram-integration-disintegration/

Type Evolution. (December 2, 2017). *The Differences Between 4w3 and 4w5 (Enneagram Wings).* https://typevolution.com/2017/12/02/the-differences-between-4w5-and-4w3/

Yuan, L. (September 10, 2019). *Here's How You Communicate, Based on Your Enneagram Type.* Psychology Junkie. https://www.psychologyjunkie.com/2019/09/10/heres-how-you-communicate-based-on-your-enneagram-type/

Part II

The Enneagram Institute. (2021). *The Enneagram Type Combinations.* https://www.enneagraminstitute.com/the-enneagram-type-combinations

Nguyen, J. (June 24, 2020). *Which Enneagram Types Go Well Together in Relationships?* Mind Body Green. https://www.mindbodygreen.com/articles/enneagram-compatibility-how-types-pair-romantically

Palmer, H. (1995). *The Enneagram in Love and Work: Understanding Your Intimate and Business Relationships*. HarperOne.

Stabile, S. (2018). *The Path Between Us: An Enneagram Journey to Healthy Relationships*. IVP Books.